Collins

Integrated Science 1

for the **Caribbean**

Gene Samuel & Derek McMonagle

Advisors:

**Shameem Narine, Nadine Victor-Ayers,
Ishaq Mohammed, Sheldon Rivas & Doltan Ramsubeik**

updated

Collins

HarperCollins*Publishers* Ltd
The News Building
1 London Bridge Street
London SE1 9GF

HarperCollins*Publishers*
Macken House, 39/40 Mayor Street Upper,
Dublin 1, D01 C9W8, Ireland

Updated edition 2017

10 9

This book contains FSC™ certified paper and other controlled
sources to ensure responsible forest management.

For more information visit: www.harpercollins.co.uk/green

ISBN 978-0-00-826308-9

www.collins.co.uk/caribbeanschools

A catalogue record for this book is available from the British Library.

Typeset by QBS Learning
Printed in India by Multivista Global Pvt. Ltd.

Authors: Gene Samuel & Derek McMonagle
Advisors: Shameem Narine, Nadine Victor-Ayers, Ishaq Mohammed, Sheldon Rivas & Doltan Ramsubeik
Illustrators: QBS Learning
Publisher: Elaine Higgleton
Commissioning Editor: Tom Hardy
Project Management: QBS Learning
Editor: Julianna Dunn
Copy Editor: Helius
Proofreader: David Hemsley
Cover Design: Gordon MacGilp

Gene Samuel has taught science at Forms 1 and 2 level at St. Joseph's Convent Secondary School, Castries,
St Lucia and is a very experienced science teacher. She has been developing resources for use in her own school
for many years.

Derek McMonagle is a leading writer of science educational materials with world-wide experience. He has
developed courses at primary, secondary and advanced levels for many countries including Jamaica and the UK.

Contents

Download your digital copy at
collins.co.uk/international-caribbean-resources

Introduction – How to use this book

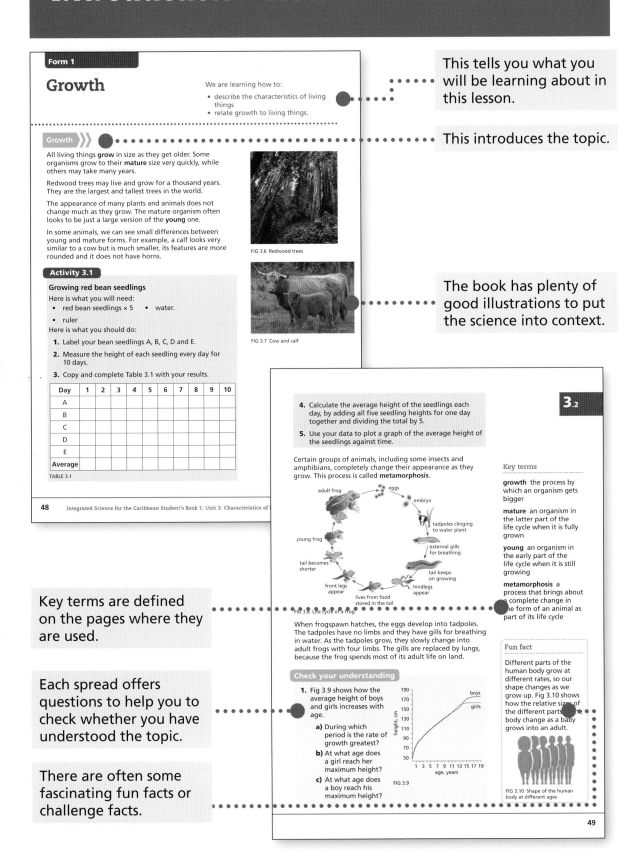

This tells you what you will be learning about in this lesson.

This introduces the topic.

The book has plenty of good illustrations to put the science into context.

Key terms are defined on the pages where they are used.

Each spread offers questions to help you to check whether you have understood the topic.

There are often some fascinating fun facts or challenge facts.

The following is the text shown in the illustrated spread:

Form 1

Growth

We are learning how to:
- describe the characteristics of living things
- relate growth to living things.

Growth

All living things **grow** in size as they get older. Some organisms grow to their **mature** size very quickly, while others may take many years.

Redwood trees may live and grow for a thousand years. They are the largest and tallest trees in the world.

The appearance of many plants and animals does not change much as they grow. The mature organism often looks to be just a large version of the **young** one.

In some animals, we can see small differences between young and mature forms. For example, a calf looks very similar to a cow but is much smaller, its features are more rounded and it does not have horns.

FIG 3.6 Redwood trees

FIG 3.7 Cow and calf

Activity 3.1

Growing red bean seedlings

Here is what you will need:
- red bean seedlings × 5
- water.
- ruler

Here is what you should do:

1. Label your bean seedlings A, B, C, D and E.
2. Measure the height of each seedling every day for 10 days.
3. Copy and complete Table 3.1 with your results.

Day	1	2	3	4	5	6	7	8	9	10
A										
B										
C										
D										
E										
Average										

TABLE 3.1

3.2

4. Calculate the average height of the seedlings each day, by adding all five seedling heights for one day together and dividing the total by 5.
5. Use your data to plot a graph of the average height of the seedlings against time.

Certain groups of animals, including some insects and amphibians, completely change their appearance as they grow. This process is called **metamorphosis**.

adult frog — eggs — embryo — tadpoles clinging to water plant — external gills for breathing — tail keeps on growing — hindlegs appear — lives from food stored in the tail — front legs appear — tail becomes shorter — young frog

FIG 3.8 Life cycle of a frog

When frogspawn hatches, the eggs develop into tadpoles. The tadpoles have no limbs and they have gills for breathing in water. As the tadpoles grow, they slowly change into adult frogs with four limbs. The gills are replaced by lungs, because the frog spends most of its adult life on land.

Check your understanding

1. Fig 3.9 shows how the average height of boys and girls increases with age.
   a) During which period is the rate of growth greatest?
   b) At what age does a girl reach her maximum height?
   c) At what age does a boy reach his maximum height?

FIG 3.9

Key terms

growth the process by which an organism gets bigger

mature an organism in the latter part of the life cycle when it is fully grown

young an organism in the early part of the life cycle when it is still growing

metamorphosis a process that brings about a complete change in the form of an animal as part of its life cycle

Fun fact

Different parts of the human body grow at different rates, so our shape changes as we grow up. Fig 3.10 shows how the relative sizes of the different parts of the body change as a baby grows into an adult.

FIG 3.10 Shape of the human body at different ages

49

Review of Science and safety in science

- Science covers a wide variety of studies, divided into branches such as astronomy, chemistry and medicine.
- Science is the systematic study of nature and the environment, through the 'scientific method'.
- Technology is the application of knowledge gained from science in practical ways, in order to improve the quality of life.
- Scientific knowledge is also used to help people make informed decisions.
- The scientific method involves making careful observations and recording and analysing data.
- Scientific skills are essential for accurate results.
- Before experimenting, scientists make hypotheses to guide their course of action.
- After experimenting, scientists record their work in a structured report.
- Carefully annotated diagrams are an important part of a scientific report.
- Scientists use a wide range of special equipment, called 'apparatus'.
- Care and the correct procedure must be observed when using a Bunsen burner
- There are safety hazards in a science laboratory, and workers must take precautions.
- Laboratory rules are written to keep workers as safe as possible.
- Safety symbols give guidance on hazards, especially when handling chemicals.

Review questions on Science and safety in science

1. What is the link between science and technology?

2. **a)** Unscramble the following branches of science:
   GOOBILY   THERMYSIC   ROOMANTYS   OLEGGOY
   SHICSPY   TAYBON   CIDIMEEN   SCHAMEMIT
   b) Pick four of these branches of science and say what is studied i

3. Give four examples of how scientific discoveries have benefited th

4. State what type of information goes into the following parts of a report:
   aim   apparatus   method   results   discussion   conclusi

At the end of each group of Units there are pages which list the key topics covered in the Units. These will be useful for revision.

At the end of each section there are special questions to help you and your teacher review your knowledge, see if you can apply this knowledge and if you can use the science skills that you have developed.

Science, Technology, Education and Mathematics (STEM) activities are included which present real-life problems to be investigated and resolved using your science and technology skills. These pages are called **Science in practice**.

Science in practice

Estimating the sugar content of sweet potato

Sweet potatoes are a popular food in the Caribbean. They are eaten in lots of different ways, including boiled, mashed, baked and as fries.

100 g of sweet potato contains about 20 g of carbohydrates, 1.6 g of protein and 0.1 g fat. It is also a good source of vitamins A, B_6, B_{12}, C and D, and of the minerals calcium, iron and magnesium.

As the name 'sweet potato' suggests, a proportion of the 20 g of carbohydrates is present as sugar. This information will be useful to someone wanting to reduce their sugar intake.

FIG 6.20 Sweet potatoes

1. You are going to work in groups of three or four to estimate the concentration of sugar in sweet potatoes using osmosis. Your tasks are:
   - to revise the work carried out on osmosis in this unit so that you understand the process
   - to prepare sugar solutions of different concentrations
   - to measure the mass gain or mass loss when sweet potato chips are soaked in sugar solutions of different concentrations
   - to draw a graph of mass gain/loss against concentration and use it to deduce the sugar concentration in sweet potatoes.

   a) Osmosis is a special kind of diffusion involving water molecules. When solutions of different concentrations are separated by a differentially permeable membrane there is a net movement of water molecules from the less concentrated solution to the more concentrated solution. Eventually the solutions will have the same concentration.

   Read through the work you carried out in Topic 6.2 Osmosis to make sure that you understand this process.

   b) Make up sugar solutions of different concentrations. The percentage of sugar in sweet potato is between 0 and 10% so you should make up solutions of 0%, 1%, ..., 10% by mass of sugar.

   To make up each solution:
   - Place a clean, dry 250 cm³ beaker on a balance.
   - Press the tare/zero key to zero the display.
   - Add sugar to the required mass.
   - Top up with distilled water until the display reads 100 g.

FIG 6.21 Making up solutions

Unit 1: Science and scientific processes

We are learning how to:
• define science and technology.

Science and technology »

What is science?

Science is the study of nature and the environment. The word 'science' comes from the Latin *scientia*, meaning 'knowledge'. In science, **observations** and **experiments** are used to describe and explain natural occurrences. The knowledge gained is never complete, but is always being added to through further research and experiments.

The various branches of science are categorised as either social sciences or natural sciences. All your activities and research will be confined to areas in the natural sciences.

FIG 1.1 A scientist at work

Activity 1.1

Finding out about different sciences

Here is what you should do:

1. Fig 1.2 identifies some natural sciences.

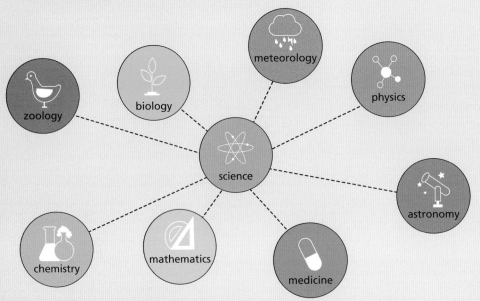

FIG 1.2 Some branches of science

In a group, discuss what is studied in each one of the sciences.

2. Match each branch of science with one area of study from the list below:

- healing
- living things
- objects beyond the Earth
- quantity
- animals
- the atmosphere
- behaviour of matter
- structure of matter.

What is technology?

The word **'technology'** comes from the Greek word *techne*, meaning 'art' or 'skill'. Technology is the **application** of knowledge gained from science in practical ways – to solve problems and improve the quality of life. Using technology, people are able to control and adapt to their natural environments. Our development and use of tools, the building of ships, and the invention of medical devices such as X-ray and MRI scanners are all examples of technology.

How does the scientific process work?

Science is not just about collecting facts to describe the natural world and its origin. It seeks to understand and then provide models for how the world works. Despite its usefulness, science has numerous limitations. For example, although science can provide guidelines to help in the recovery from the passage of a hurricane, it is unable to stop the action of a hurricane. These limitations are used as stepping stones for acquiring even more knowledge with which to address new issues – an example is the creation of hurricane braces to attach roofs more securely to houses.

FIG 1.3 A doctor using an MRI scanner

Fun fact

The first wristwatch was made by Patek Philippe in 1868.

Key terms

science system for studying the physical and living worlds based on experiments

observation collecting information via the senses

experiment the process of conducting a scientific test

technology the use of knowledge gained from science experiments to improve the quality of life

application putting scientific information to special use

Check your understanding

1. Explain the difference between science and technology. Give some examples of scientific discovery and of technological developments.

2. Find out what made each of the following scientists famous:

- Thomas Edison
- Richard Leakey
- Isaac Newton
- Jane Goodall
- Marie Curie
- John Dalton
- Maria Goeppert-Mayer
- Albert Einstein
- Louis Pasteur.

FIG 1.4 Famous scientists:
a) Maria Goeppert-Mayer and
b) Albert Einstein

Impacts of science and technology

We are learning how to:

- make use of science and technology to solve community-based issues.

Impact of science and technology on daily life ⟩⟩⟩

Science and technology influence life today in a huge variety of ways. Imagine your day:

- You are awoken at 6 a.m. by the music from your clock radio. You jump down from your bunk bed and into your bedroom slippers. You rush to the bathroom, turn on the light and the heater and have a shower. You iron your shirt, get dressed and comb your hair while looking in the mirror.

- Then you go to the kitchen, grab the remote control and turn on the television. You switch on the coffee maker and toaster, and while your coffee is brewing and your bread is toasting you select your cutlery and crockery. You go to the fridge and find the ingredients for your packed lunch.

- After breakfast, you clean up the kitchen, change the water in your pet bird's cage and put out the rubbish as the bin lorry passes.

All of these aspects of life are influenced by science and technology, which have also contributed to the development of motor vehicles, telephone lines, lifts, space rockets and water-treatment plants and, on a smaller scale, items like washers for tap heads, aglets (metal or plastic tube fixed around each end of a shoelace) and paperclips.

FIG 1.5 Some of our daily activities

Activity 1.2

Group work for class presentation

Here is what you should do:

1. Interview an elderly person and find out how life was for them growing up: the type of recreation activities there were, food, houses, communication, etc. Compare their lifestyle with that of today.

2. Compare how telecommunication services worked in the past and how they have been developed to what they are today.

3. Compare the transport service, from horseback to space travel.

4. Consider the invention of gadgets (for example, a bottle opener) to make work easier.

Despite all these advantages of scientific and technological progress, there can be disadvantages. The demand for paper, wood and rubber reduces the number of trees. Fuels for cars and factories cause pollution. Medication can be accompanied by side effects. The important thing to note here is that technological solutions to scientific problems must be applied carefully and with the proper precautions.

Science and technology are also applied widely in medicine, agriculture, defence, economics, leisure and exploration. It does not seem that there is any barrier to the current rate of technological advancement.

Check your understanding

1. List two advantages and two disadvantages of the smartphone.

2. List two advantages and two disadvantages of modern cars.

Fun fact

FIG 1.6

In 1968, the first computer mouse was introduced by Douglas Engelbart at a Computer Expo in the USA.

Scientific skills

We are learning how to:

- use scientific skills to carry out an experiment using the scientific method.

The scientific method >>

Scientists carry out their work or research in an organised, or systematic, way called the **scientific method**. Why is it necessary for scientists to be so organised?

To become a scientist, you need to develop a number of skills to enable you to carry out research that gives accurate results. Inaccurate results give a false picture of the subject under research. It is therefore important for scientists to be very careful and organised.

The table below gives five scientific skills and their definitions. You will develop these skills as you work through this course.

FIG 1.7 An agricultural scientist at work

Skill	Definition
Hypothesising	Suggesting a possible explanation for things in a way that can be tested
Planning and conducting experiments	Carrying out a process to answer a specific question
Collecting data	Gathering numerical information
Recording and reporting	Ensuring data is written down securely and then presenting it in tables, diagrams or charts so that it is easily understood
Analysing data	Looking for patterns and information within sets of data

TABLE 1.1 Scientific skills

Scientists use all the skills listed in Table 1.1 when they conduct experiments.

Experimenting scientifically

You will carry out an experiment on piercing balloons.

Scientists always have a reason for carrying out an experiment. Now think of what you will do and why – suppose you place sticky tape on the balloon and pierce through the tape, what **prediction** can you make?

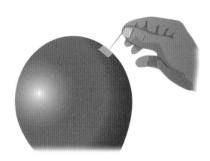

FIG 1.8

When the experiment is completed you will write a report, so you must be extremely observant during the experiment.

Before conducting an experiment, it is important that you check that:

- everything you need to use is available and close at hand
- you have carefully read and understood all instructions.

Activity 1.3

Here is what you need:

- balloons
- clear sticky tape
- a straight pin
- scissors.

Here is what you should do:

1. Inflate two balloons fully and tie each one at the neck.

2. Pierce one of the balloons with the pin. Do not let go of the pin. Carefully observe what happens.

3. Place sticky tape on the other balloon so that there are no air pockets between the tape and the balloon.

4. Pierce this balloon through the tape. Do not let go of the pin. Carefully observe what happens.

5. Record what you observed with both balloons.

6. Provide suggestions to explain what you observed.

Check your understanding

1. Why did you have to hold on to the pin?

2. Why was it important that there were no air pockets between the tape and the balloon?

3. What caused the first balloon to burst so quickly?

4. Was the behaviour of the air in both balloons the same or different?

5. Give a reason to support your answer.

Fun fact

The microwave oven was invented by a researcher who, when he walked past a radar tube, found that the chocolate bar in his pocket melted.

Key terms

scientific method the systematic manner of conducting experiments

hypothesising making statements in such a way that they can be verified

planning formulating an orderly set of events which may lead to achieving a goal

analysing explaining the reason for the method used and the steps taken to limit errors

predicting stating expected outcomes based on experience

Writing a lab report

We are learning how to:

- write a report on a scientific experiment.

Experimental reports

Whenever scientists carry out their experiments they record each section using a particular format. This is called a **lab report**. It is necessary for budding scientists to learn the correct method for writing reports.

Format for writing a report

Title: Give the name of the experiment.

Date: State when you did it.

Aim: State what you are intending to achieve.

Apparatus and materials: Identify all the tools and items to be used. This section may include diagrams of how to set up the apparatus.

Method/procedure: Record the steps of the experiment:

- use the past tense
- write the steps in order
- number the steps.

The method may include diagrams.

Observation/results: Record what happens – anything you see, hear or smell (or, in some experiments, taste) – and any measurements. Use tables and graphs. You may include annotated diagrams.

Analysis and discussion: Discuss your observations. Explain what these show.

Sources of error: Consider all the possible sources of error in your readings. Which ones are important?

Precautions taken: Explain the steps you took to limit errors.

Conclusion: Draw inferences from the experiments based on the aim.

Reflections: Did your investigation give useful results? Does it suggest a way forward for further investigations?

FIG 1.9

Activity 1.4

Writing a report

Here is what you should do:

1. Now that you know the format for writing a report on an experiment, see how well you can write up a report on your balloon experiment. Make sure that your report is neat and well laid out. You can use a computer if one is available.

Practising report-writing skills

It requires practice to become a scientist. Hence, in this course, there will be many opportunities for carrying out and **recording** experiments.

FIG 1.10

Check your understanding

1. Below are some excerpts from lab reports. Say in which section they would be in a lab report.

   a) A container was filled with oil and another container was filled with water. A new iron nail was placed in each container and left for a week.

   b) A metre rule was used to measure the heights of all the plants.

   c) When the freezer was opened, it was found that all the containers were cracked.

   d) The water expanded when the ice was formed.

   e) Since both lids A and B were the same size, the heat had caused lid A to expand.

2. In a lab report, the Aim may include predictions. Which section tells whether a prediction is correct?

Key terms

lab report A report of a scientific investigation or experiment in a standard format

aim stating what is being explored and making any prediction(s)

apparatus the tools and equipment that scientists use

method a written record of the steps of an experiment

analysis an explanation of or the reason for the method used and of the steps taken to limit errors

conclusion a deduction made based on information gathered

recording writing down information, which can be used or seen again

Making scientific drawings

We are learning how to:

- draw scientific diagrams.

Scientific diagrams 》》

When scientists record the apparatus used and observations made in an experiment, they often need to draw diagrams. Producing diagrams in science does not require special art skills. There are, however, some basic guidelines for making scientific drawings, which are outlined below.

- All scientific drawings must be as simple as possible but also as true to life as possible.

- Drawings must be done in pencil – no coloured pens or markers should be used.

- Sharp pencils and a ruler, eraser and sharpener are needed.

- Various pencil techniques are used for natural objects. You should draw:
  - ○ smooth-edged specimens using smooth unbroken lines
  - ○ specimens of wool, cotton or hair with fuzzy edges
  - ○ underlying structures with broken lines (to indicate their shape).

- No shading is done. Other techniques are used:
  - ○ stippling (dotting)
  - ○ streaking (lines in one direction)
  - ○ cross-hatching (lines crossing each other).

FIG 1.11 This drawing of a plant uses colour and shading; these are not needed for scientific diagrams

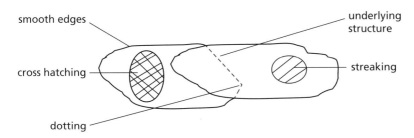

FIG 1.12 Some of the drawing techniques used in science

- **Symbols** may be used if their meaning is made clear.

Activity 1.5

Drawing a leaf

Here is what you need:

- a simple-shaped leaf that is neither too small nor too large

- drawing materials.

Here is what you should do:

1. Place the leaf on the desk so that you do not have to move it while you draw.

2. Draw the outline of your leaf in the middle of your page. Your drawing should have no sketchy edges and look as smooth and sharp as in Fig 1.13.

FIG 1.13 Outline of a simple leaf

Do not discard the leaf.

Your teacher will assess your drawing and guide you to complete the diagram, which may look like the leaf in Fig 1.14.

FIG 1.14 Drawing of a simple leaf

Check your understanding

1. A student drew this picture of a flower. List three good points about this drawing and then list three bad points.

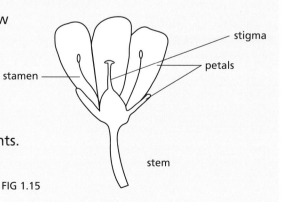

FIG 1.15

2. Explain why label lines should be straight.

Fun fact

The falling of autumn leaves is extremely important to the ecological balance of the environment. The dropped leaves help to form the organic layer of the soil surface, and the nutrients in the leaves are recycled by decomposers.

Key term

symbol a character or drawing used to represent a situation

Labelling scientific diagrams

We are learning how to:

- label scientific diagrams
- work out the magnification of a diagram.

Annotating a diagram »»

Scientific drawings need to be **annotated** – labelled with descriptive words. There are some rules to follow when labelling a diagram.

- **Title**:
  - ○ indicates what the diagram represents
  - ○ is best written in CAPITAL letters
  - ○ is best placed at the bottom centre of the drawing.
- **Labels**:
  - ○ identify the various parts of the drawing
  - ○ are written in pencil
  - ○ are either all small letters or all CAPITAL letters, but not a mixture.
- **Labelling lines**:
  - ○ are drawn horizontally wherever possible
  - ○ are drawn in pencil using a ruler
  - ○ should connect to the drawings
  - ○ do not have arrowheads or dots at either end
  - ○ end on the part or in the space they identify
  - ○ do not cross over each other.
- For biological drawings of natural objects, the **magnification** and the view (for example, plan view – from the front, side view – in profile, or cross-section – cut through and showing the cut edge) of the drawing are written close to the title.

Activity 1.6

Labelling your leaf diagram

Here is what you need:

- your leaf diagram from Activity 1.5.

Here is what you should do:

1. Label your leaf diagram. (Your teacher will guide you to do this correctly.)

2. When you have labelled your leaf diagram, it should look like the following:

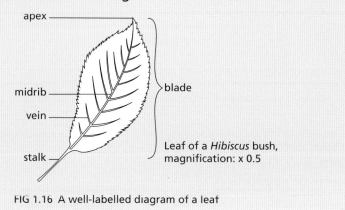

apex

midrib

vein

blade

stalk

Leaf of a *Hibiscus* bush, magnification: x 0.5

FIG 1.16 A well-labelled diagram of a leaf

Calculating the magnification

If the diagram is bigger than the **specimen**, do you think the magnification will be larger or smaller than 1? (Hint: the actual specimen is always rated 1.)

Place the specimen over the drawing and judge how many times the specimen can fit into the drawing.

To find out the magnification of your diagram:

1. Measure the length or the width of both the specimen and your drawing.

2. Divide the dimension of your drawing by that of the specimen. The result is the magnification.

$$\text{magnification} = \frac{\text{length of drawing}}{\text{length of object}}$$

Check your understanding

1. Fig 1.17(a) represents a specimen (a dissected frog). Fig 1.17(b) is a diagram of the specimen. Work out the magnification.

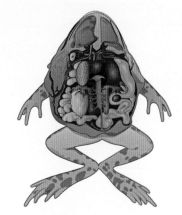

FIG 1.17 **a)** A dissected frog

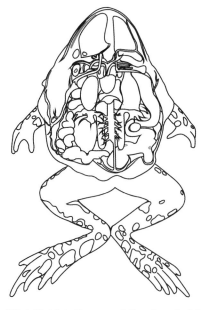

FIG 1.17 **b)** A diagram of the dissected frog

Fun fact

It is not necessary for frogs to drink water because they absorb water through their skin.

Key terms

annotated having important or explanatory notes

magnification the scalar representation of an actual specimen

specimen the item or material under examination

Scientific apparatus

We are learning how to:

- identify and draw some common apparatus used in school science lessons
- use a Bunsen burner.

Apparatus for scientists ▷▷▷

As with all workers, scientists have special tools for their jobs. These tools and equipment are called 'apparatus'. There are dozens of pieces of apparatus, each with its own unique use.

Test-tube rack

Activity 1.7

Getting familiar with apparatus

Here is what you should do:

1. Your teacher will show you some pieces of apparatus. See whether you can guess what the different pieces of apparatus are used for.

2. Practise drawing items of apparatus, and learn their names and uses.

Safety glasses

Reagent bottle

Fig 1.18 shows some scientific apparatus.

Bunsen burner

Evaporating dish

Conical flask

Round-bottomed flask

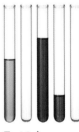
Test tube

Filter funnel

Beaker

Electronic balance

Measuring cylinder

Stand and clamp

FIG 1.18 Some scientific apparatus

Each piece of apparatus shown in Fig 1.18 has a particular use and function:

- **Test tube or boiling tube** – for containing (maybe for heating) small amounts of substances.
- **Beaker** – for containing chemicals or collecting liquids
- **Measuring cylinder** – for measuring accurately the volume of liquids.
- **Round-bottomed flask** – for the preparation of gases if the process requires heating.
- **Conical flask** – for the preparation of gases if no heating is required.
- **Filter funnel** – for separating an insoluble solid from a liquid with the help of filter paper.
- **Evaporating dish** – for evaporating a liquid from a solution.
- **Crucible** – for heating solids over a flame.
- **Tripod stand** – for supporting apparatus during heating.
- **Stand and clamp** – for supporting apparatus during experiments.
- **Bunsen burner** – to provide a flame for heating.
- **Safety glasses** – to protect your eyes while experimenting.

Bunsen burner

Your teacher will demonstrate and explain the correct procedure for lighting a **Bunsen burner**, and will show and explain the difference between a **luminous flame** and a **non-luminous flame**.

Fun fact

Mechanical lighters were used before matches were invented.

Key terms

Bunsen burner apparatus which provides heat – named after its inventor

luminous flame a warm, yellow flame burning with incomplete combustion

non-luminous flame a bright, very hot, blue Bunsen flame which burns with complete combustion, producing water and carbon dioxide

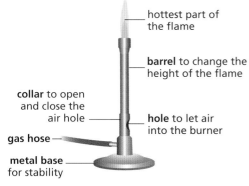

FIG 1.19 The parts of a Bunsen burner and their functions

hottest part of the flame

barrel to change the height of the flame

collar to open and close the air hole

hole to let air into the burner

gas hose

metal base for stability

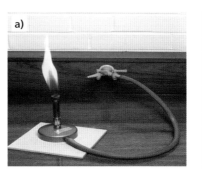

FIG 1.20 Bunsen burner flames: **a)** luminous and **b)** non-luminous

Activity 1.8

Understanding apparatus

1. Find out who the Bunsen burner was named after.

2. Explain what you would use a Bunsen burner for. When might it be dangerous to use a Bunsen burner?

Safety in science

We are learning how to:

- interpret safety symbols.

Safety symbols ⟩⟩⟩

There are many safety **hazards** in a science laboratory ('lab'), including many types of chemical. Different chemicals pose different risks. There are internationally recognised symbols designed specifically for lab safety, especially when handling chemicals.

Activity 1.9

Looking at safety symbols found on chemical containers

1. Fig 1.21 shows the seven common safety symbols. Can you match them with what they represent from the list of words?

| 1 | 2 | 3 |

| toxic | oxidising | radioactive | corrosive |
| explosive | flammable | irritant/harmful | |

| 4 | 5 | 6 | 7 |

FIG 1.21 Safety symbols

2. Your teacher will show you bottles and containers with symbols. Test your memory by identifying the symbols on them.

3. Draw the safety symbols in your lab book/note book or download and print them out. Then write what each one means.

Activity 1.10

What would you do?

Here is what you should do:

1. In a group, role-play a scenario of what could happen if someone comes in contact with a chemical after ignoring its safety symbol, and what should be done.

FIG 1.22 Safety symbols are provided on domestic cleaning agents

Check your understanding

1. Check the labels of various products at home and identify the safety symbols. Identify which component of each product most influences the care that should be taken when using it.

2. Carry out research and explain what would happen if someone mixed a product that contains chlorine with another that contains ammonia.

Fun fact

In Victoria, Australia, many people believe that unless you're a qualified electrician, it's illegal under Victorian law to change a light bulb in your own home - and doing so will attract a $10 fine. This was the case but the law was amended in 1999 to make the changing of a light bulb exempt.

Key terms

hazard an unavoidable danger or risk

toxic poisonous

oxidising providing oxygen so that substances can burn or react in other ways

corrosive destroys substances by wearing them away while chemically reacting with them

irritant substance that is neither corrosive nor toxic but reacts negatively on contact

flammable ignites easily

precaution safety measure

Safety in the school laboratory

We are learning how to:

- behave properly whenever we are in the lab
- carry out lab activities
- work in an orderly and careful way
- react if accidents occur.

Working safely ≫

The **laboratory** is the special place where scientists carry out their work. It is usually referred to as the 'lab'. As budding scientists, it is necessary that you know the rules of conduct that govern all lab activity so that you are always safe when carrying out activities.

Activity 1.11

Recognising unsafe activities

Examine the picture in Fig 1.23. Say which activities you think should not be done in the lab. Explain why not.

FIG 1.23

General lab rules

These general rules should be followed when working in the lab:

1. Permission is needed to enter the lab.

2. No food or drink should be brought into the lab.

3. Open all doors and windows unless otherwise directed.

4. Always walk in the lab. Do not run or play around.

5. Store all coats, bags and other belongings tidily.

6. Do not tamper with any electrical mains or fittings.

7. Do not attempt experiments without the teacher's permission.

8. Read all instructions carefully and ask for clarification as required.

9. Handle apparatus and materials both carefully and correctly.

10. Report immediately any broken or damaged apparatus.

11. Do not remove apparatus or chemicals from the lab.

12. Work tidily, clean all apparatus thoroughly and dispose of waste correctly.

13. Do not hold hot apparatus with your bare hands.

14. Wash hands thoroughly before leaving the lab or experimenting.

When accidents occur:

- Report all accidents, injuries, breakages or spillages to your teacher immediately.

- If a chemical gets into your mouth, spit it into a container and rinse your mouth as quickly as possible with plenty of water and report the incident to the teacher.

- If any chemical falls on your body or clothing, rinse the area thoroughly with water and report the incident to the teacher.

Check your understanding

1. Say why it is necessary to have lab rules.

2. Give three rules that need to be followed whenever you are in the lab.

3. Why should you not pour unused chemicals back into the bottles?

4. List some accidents that may occur in the lab.

Lab rules

We can summarise the way we should act in the lab in five simple rules that you should remember: four 'Don'ts' and one 'Do'.

- **Don't** come into the lab until you are told to do so by your teacher.

- **Don't** touch apparatus and chemicals you might see in the lab unless instructed to do so by your teacher.

- **Don't** run about or mess around in the lab.

- **Don't** eat or drink in the lab.

- **Do** report any accident to your teacher, no matter how small.

Key term

laboratory a room used for scientific experiments

Review of Science and safety in science

- Science covers a wide variety of studies, divided into branches such as astronomy, chemistry and medicine.

- Science is the systematic study of nature and the environment, through the 'scientific method'.

- Technology is the application of knowledge gained from science in practical ways, in order to improve the quality of life.

- Scientific knowledge is also used to help people make informed decisions.

- The scientific method involves making careful observations and recording and analysing data.

- Scientific skills are essential for accurate results.

- Before experimenting, scientists make hypotheses to guide their course of action.

- After experimenting, scientists record their work in a structured report.

- Carefully annotated diagrams are an important part of a scientific report.

- Scientists use a wide range of special equipment, called 'apparatus'.

- Care and the correct procedure must be observed when using a Bunsen burner.

- There are safety hazards in a science laboratory, and workers must take precautions.

- Laboratory rules are written to keep workers as safe as possible.

- Safety symbols give guidance on hazards, especially when handling chemicals.

Review questions on Science and safety in science

1. What is the link between science and technology?

2. **a)** Unscramble the following branches of science:

   GOOBILY   THERMYSIC   ROOMANTYS   OLEGGOY

   SHICSPY   TAYBON   CIDIMEEN   SCHAMEMITTA

   b) Pick four of these branches of science and say what is studied in each.

3. Give four examples of how scientific discoveries have benefited the world.

4. State what type of information goes into the following parts of an experimental report:

   aim   apparatus   method   results   discussion   conclusion

5. Sandy carried out an experiment in which she placed one nail in water and one in oil. She found that after one week the nail in water had rusted while the one in oil had not. The oil had sealed the nail in, preventing air from contacting the nail. Write up, as an experimental report, how Sandy might have carried this experiment out and how she came to this conclusion.

6. Jan, a Form 1 science student, has drawn and labelled the diagram of a cell, as shown on the right. However, she did not follow all the labelling guidelines used in science. Identify as many things as you can that show she did not follow the guidelines.

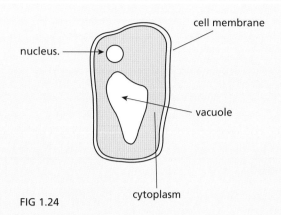

FIG 1.24

7. For each piece of lab apparatus in Fig 1.25, next to its number write its name and give its use.

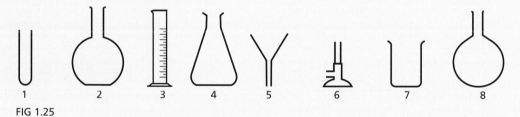

FIG 1.25

8. Make annotated drawings to show that you can recognise the difference between a luminous and a non-luminous Bunsen burner flame.

9. Label the parts of the Bunsen burner indicated in Fig 1.26.

10. The following is a scenario that occurred one morning at school. Identify five activities that were done wrongly.

One morning, as soon as the bell rang, Ms Jade's enthusiastic students rushed down to the science lab, as they were all excited to begin their work. They entered the lab before the teacher arrived and started their experiments. Soon the light bulbs began to flicker. One student opened the switch box to investigate the problem. Suddenly, all the lights went off. As it was dark, the students took all the apparatus and materials outside and continued their experiments. When the bell rang for breaktime, they immediately stopped working, left their equipment and hurried back to their classroom. They had brought their breaktime snacks to the lab with them, so they ate them on the way back.

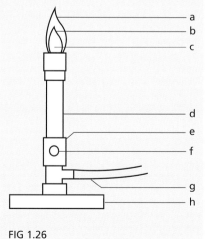

FIG 1.26

Unit 2: Scientific measurement and SI units

We are learning how to:

- state what measuring is and why we need to measure
- use standard units.

What is measuring and why do we measure? 〉〉〉

Measuring is the means by which the size, mass and/or temperature of some quantity of matter, or a period of time, is determined using **instruments** marked in **standard units**.

It is necessary to measure so that communication about any quantity of matter is clear.

The main **physical quantities** that can be measured are:

- Dimensions – the size of an object in terms of, for example, its length, width, height or depth.
- Volume – how much space an object occupies.
- Mass – how much matter an object contains.
- Time – how long an event lasts.
- Temperature – how hot an object is.

FIG 2.1 How far is it to Chaguanas?

It's not far to Chaguanas – it's about 250 pieces of string away.

Units of measurement

We need to have standard units of measurement so that we can make useful comparisons. In science, we use mostly **SI units**. The different SI units are shown in Table 2.1.

Physical quantity	SI unit	Symbol	Instrument(s)
length	metre	m	metre rule, tape measure, calliper
mass	kilogram	kg	balance
time	second	s	stopwatch, clock
temperature	kelvin	K	thermometer

TABLE 2.1 Some SI units of measurement, their symbols and the instrument(s) used

FIG 2.2 A thermometer

Other units are also used, such as degrees Celsius (°C) for temperature and minutes for time.

Multiples and submultiples of SI units have names;
for example:

1 kilometre = 1000 metres or 1 km = 1000 m

1 centimetre = 1/100 metre or 1 cm = 1/100 m

1 millimetre = 1/1000 metre or 1 mm = 1/1000 m

Square centimetres and cubic centimetres are often used for the area and volume of everyday objects, as shown in Table 2.2.

The volume of a liquid is often measured in litres (l) and millilitres (ml). One millilitre (1 ml) is equal to one cubic centimetre (cm^3).

Physical quantity	Unit	Symbol
area	square centimetre	cm^2
volume	cubic centimetre	cm^3

TABLE 2.2

Activity 2.1

How good are you at estimating?

Here is what you need:

- rulers
- tape measures
- metre rules
- stopwatches
- balances.

Here is what you should do:

1. In groups, test each other's skills at **estimating** the lengths and masses of various objects, and the time taken for short activities such as walking a few paces.

2. Use an appropriate measuring instrument to check your estimates.

3. Back in class, discuss the techniques you used to estimate values and how good your estimates were.

Estimating is a useful skill, but our senses are not reliable. Each person's ability to judge a physical property is different. As a result, it is necessary to use specially designed measuring instruments and standard units that give us the information consistently and globally.

Check your understanding

1. Explain why standard units of measurement are needed.

2. How many millilitres are there in one litre?

3. What instrument do we use in the laboratory to measure the volume of a liquid? What might we use in the kitchen at home?

4. What unit of mass is 1/1000 of a kilogram?

> **Fun fact**
>
> Yonge Street in Toronto, Canada, is the longest street in the world. It measures 1896 km (1178 miles).

Key terms

measuring using instruments to determine quantities

instrument a tool used for measuring

standard unit a value that can be communicated universally

physical quantity an amount that can be measured

SI units international system of units of measurement

estimate a calculated approximation

Measuring length

We are learning how to:

• measure as accurately as possible using a ruler.

Accuracy >>>

Measurement, unlike estimation, needs to be **accurate**.

Activity 2.2

Using your ruler

Here is what you need:

• ruler

• textbook.

Here is what you should do:

1. Look at your ruler. In what units is the scale?

2. Pick two consecutive numbers on your ruler's scale. How many small divisions are there between the two?

3. What is the length of each division?

4. Measure the length of your textbook using your ruler. Remember to give the units.

5. Suppose the end of your ruler was broken off – would you know what to do?

If the zero mark of a ruler is worn away or broken off, there are two ways of getting the value of a length:

• Consider the starting point of the object's length to be 0. Then count the next number as 1, then 2, and so on.

• Subtract the start point of the object on the ruler from its end point.

Activity 2.3

Evaluating your method

Here is what you need:

• ruler

• textbook.

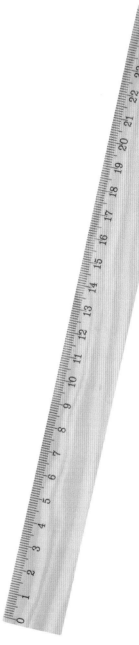

FIG 2.3

Here is what you should do:

1. When you measured the length of your textbook, how did you position the ruler and read the measurement? Why did you do it like this?

2. Place the ruler back on your textbook to measure its length again, and stand and look at the measurement from different angles. Do you get the same reading from every angle?

3. Measure another length and judge the best position from which to get the most accurate reading.

Reducing error when measuring length

To read the **scale** of a ruler, your eye must be placed vertically over the mark if the ruler is horizontal (Fig 2.4) or horizontally at the mark if the ruler is vertical. If your eye is wrongly positioned, you will obtain an **inaccurate** measurement with a **parallax error**. Reading the ruler correctly will avoid such an error.

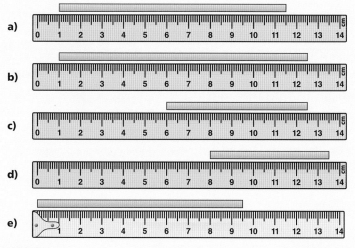

FIG 2.4 Correct and incorrect eye positions for measuring length

Check your understanding

1. In Fig 2.5 below, the ruler scales are in cm, with mm divisions. Measure the lengths of the red bars in the questions below. Give your answers in cm. Compare your answers with those of your group.

a)

b)

c)

d)

e)

FIG 2.5

2. a) Explain what is meant by a parallax error.

   b) Describe how you would avoid the parallax error if you were measuring the height of a plant.

3. Measure the length of this line.

4. Measure the length and width of this book.

Key terms

accurate free of error

scale pre-calculated set of measurements

inaccurate containing incorrect information

parallax error incorrect measurements read due to wrong eye placement

zero error incorrect measurements due to the 'zero' being set at the wrong point

Measuring length with callipers

We are learning how to:

- use a calliper to measure the length of objects
- identify objects that require a calliper to find their length
- explain the meaning of 'precise'.

Measuring length 〉〉〉

Activity 2.4

Trying different measuring instruments

Here is what you need:

- ball
- beaker
- ruler
- tape measure
- different types of calliper.

Here is what you should do:

1. To find the diameter of the ball, which instrument should you use? Try each one.

2. To find the diameter of the beaker, which instrument would you use? Suggest which is best, and why.

A **calliper** measures thickness, and is designed to hold a curved object in place as the measurement is taken (Fig 2.6). Some callipers have a built-in scale, and some even have a digital readout.

Internal and external callipers can be used to find **internal** and **external** diameters, for example of cans and beakers (Fig 2.7). They have no scale and need to be removed from the object without altering the distance between the legs. Then the calliper legs can be placed against a ruler and the length measured.

FIG 2.6 Using a calliper

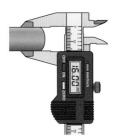

External calliper to measure external diameter

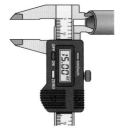

Internal calliper to measure internal diameter

FIG 2.7 Using external and internal callipers

Activity 2.5

Choosing the best instrument for the task

Here is what you need:
- ruler
- tape measure
- different types of calliper.

Here is what you should do:

1. Use the appropriate instruments to measure the dimensions of various objects around the classroom.

2. Write your measurements in a table. Allow space to record your repeat measurements. Take care with your table headings, and remember to include units.

Range and precision

Small lengths and distances need an instrument with a small **range**, such as a ruler that measures from 0 to 15 cm.

For longer lengths, an instrument with a longer range is needed. But this measuring instrument may not be as **precise**: a measuring tape that is 100 m long will probably not have millimetre divisions.

Check your understanding

1. **a)** What are the external and internal diameter measurements in Fig 2.7?

   b) Draw a cross-section of a can and label it with the measurements from **1 a)**.

   c) Which diameter measurement would you use if you wanted to calculate the volume of the can?

2. What instrument and what unit would you use to find the length of:

   a) a classroom block?

   b) a street?

3. Imagine you had two rulers, one with 1-mm divisions and one with 5-mm divisions. Explain which one will give a more precise measurement of length.

Key terms

calliper an instrument for measuring thickness that is specially designed to hold the object it is measuring in place

internal calliper an instrument for measuring the interior dimension of items

external calliper an instrument for measuring the exterior dimension of items

range the spread or width of a set of values

precise exact

Measuring volumes of liquids

We are learning how to:

- read volume accurately using a measuring cylinder.

What is volume? »»

Volume is how much space matter takes up. It may be a quantity of liquid taking up space in a container, or it may be an object like a book or a stone taking up space in the air.

Activity 2.6

Reading a measuring cylinder

Here is what you need:

- measuring cylinder
- beaker of water.

Here is what you should do:

1. Look at the scale on the measuring cylinder. How has the cylinder been numbered? What are the units? (The units will probably be ml or cm^3.)

2. Between each whole number, how many divisions are there? Give the value of each division, including the unit.

3. Using the beaker, pour some water into the measuring cylinder and observe the top surface of the water.

4. Read the volume of the water in the cylinder.

Leave the water in the measuring cylinder.

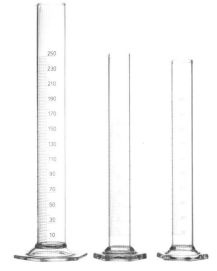

FIG 2.8 Different measuring cylinders are used to measure different quantities of liquids

When a liquid is placed in a container, it forms a curved surface called the **meniscus** (from the Greek word for crescent). The edges of the meniscus may curve either upwards (a **concave** meniscus) or downwards (a **convex** meniscus), as shown in Fig 2.9. Most liquids, including water, have a concave meniscus.

When reading the level of a liquid, you should consider the meniscus so that you obtain an accurate measurement. Read the level at the bottom of a concave meniscus or at the top of a convex meniscus. For accuracy, you must read the meniscus at eye level. This avoids parallax error (see Fig 2.9).

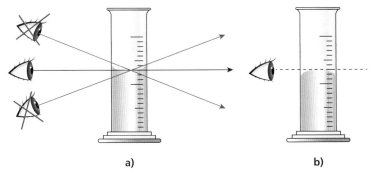

FIG 2.9 You need to read the level at **a)** the bottom of a concave meniscus or **b)** the top of a convex meniscus. Your eye should be level with the meniscus for accuracy

Key terms

volume space occupied by a three-dimensional object or substance

meniscus the curved or crescent-shaped upper surface of a column of liquid

concave curving downwards: the meniscus has a 'u' shape

convex curving upwards: the meniscus has an 'n' shape

Activity 2.7

Reading a measuring cylinder more accurately

Here is what you should do:

1. Look again at the surface of the water in your measuring cylinder. Look closely at the meniscus. With your head positioned to avoid parallax error, and looking at the bottom of the meniscus, read the volume again.

2. Do you get a different result from that in Activity 2.6?

Check your understanding

1. Read the volume of liquid in the cylinders in Fig 2.10. Remember to include the units.

FIG 2.10

2. Which measuring cylinder(s) in Fig 2.10 will give the:

   a) most precise reading?

   b) least precise reading?

(Hint: work out the value of the smallest scale divisions in each.)

Measuring the volume of an irregular solid object

We are learning how to:

* find the volume of an object.

Measuring volume 》》

To find the volume of a regularly shaped object like a book, a brick or a can, we can measure the lengths of the sides, the height and so on, and calculate the volume using formulae. How can we find the volume of an irregularly shaped object?

Since volume is the amount of space an object occupies, it is possible to find the object's volume by the amount of liquid it **displaces**. Think about what happens to the water level when you get in the bath.

Activity 2.8

Finding the volume of an irregular solid

Here is what you need:

* a stone
* large measuring cylinder and/or displacement can and small measuring cylinder
* beaker of water
* small bowl or other container
* a cloth to mop up spillages.

Here is what you should do:

1. Look at the stone and your equipment, and discuss how you could find the stone's volume as accurately as possible.

2. Follow method 1 (see Fig 2.11):

   a) Pour water into the large measuring cylinder and record its volume. Remember to use the technique that you used in Activity 2.7.

   b) Gently slide the stone into the measuring cylinder of water. What happens to the level of water? Why?

   c) Record the new volume.

   d) What do you need to do to find the volume of the stone? Do the calculation and record the volume of the stone.

3. Follow method 2 (see Fig 2.12):

   a) Stand the displacement can on a flat surface and put the small measuring cylinder under the spout.

   b) Pour water into the displacement can until it reaches the spout.

   c) Carefully place the stone into the displacement can. What do you observe?

   d) Read the final volume of water in the measuring cylinder and record it. What does this volume represent?

4. Write a report of how you found the volume of the stone. Explain which apparatus you used. Include any precautions you took. Comment on any difficulties you had.

5. If you used both methods, compare your two results for the stone's volume. If they are different, suggest why.

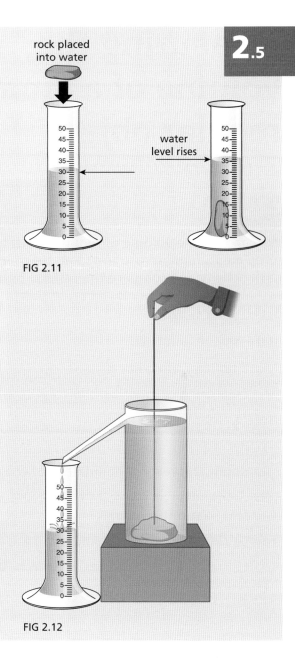

rock placed into water

water level rises

FIG 2.11

FIG 2.12

Check your understanding

1. How would you find the volume of an object that floats?

2. Suggest another way to find the volume of a regular solid object such as a cube.

3. How could you find the volume of a small coin such as a 10c piece, if you had twenty 10c pieces?

Key term

displacement the action of an object pushing liquid out of the way so that it can occupy the space

Measuring the volume of a small regular object

We are learning how to:

- find the volume of a small object by calculation
- use various methods to get the same volume of an object.

Volume 》》

We can find the volume of regular solids by displacement or by measurement. Use the same set of identical coins for each activity and compare the results.

Activity 2.9

Here is what you need:

- a number of identical coins
- measuring cylinder part-filled with water.

Here is what you should do:

1. Record the volume of water.

2. Count and record the number of coins.

3. Gently slide all the coins into the measuring cylinder and record the volume.

4. Calculate the total volume of all the coins.

5. Calculate the volume of one coin by dividing by the number of coins.

a)

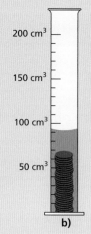

200 cm³
150 cm³
100 cm³
50 cm³

b)

FIG 2.13 **a)** A collection of identical coins and **b)** the coins placed inside a part-filled measuring cylinder

Activity 2.10

Here is what you need:

- a number of identical coins
- callipers.

Here is what you should do;

1. Use the callipers to measure the diameter of each coin (see Fig 2.14).

2. Calculate the radius of each coin and record it.

3. Using the callipers, measure the thickness of the each coin.

4. From the measurements you just made, calculate the volume of a single coin.

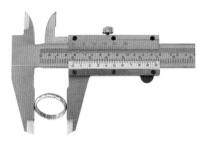

FIG 2.14

Compare the two results from the activities for the volume of one coin. Did they give the same answer? If the answers were different, can you explain why?

The volume of an object indicates the amount of space it occupies. The method used to determine the volume of an object is dependent on the shape or form of the object. If more than one method is used, the results should be the same, because the volume of the object is not changing.

Check your understanding

1. Why is it necessary to use many identical objects to determine the volume of one object when using the displacement method?

2. Why do the objects have to be identical?

3. What types of objects have dimensions that cannot be measured easily, so that their volume can only be found by displacement?

4. Name some objects with volumes that can be found by measuring the dimensions.

> **Fun fact**
>
> Of all the cuboids of the same surface area, the cube has the greatest volume.

Measuring mass

We are learning how to:

- adjust a bathroom scale and use it to measure your mass
- explain the suitability of balances.

Mass

Mass is the amount of matter in a body. It is measured in grams or kilograms.

Activity 2.11

Measuring your mass

Here is what you need:

- bathroom scales.

Here is what you should do:

1. Examine your set of bathroom scales carefully. They might look like the ones shown in Fig 2.15.

   a) Do the scales have two measurement scales or just one?

   b) What are the units of mass?

   c) How much mass does each larger division represent?

   d) How much mass does each smaller division represent?

   e) Do the scales have a zeroing knob so that they can be made to read '0' accurately when there is no mass placed on them?

FIG 2.15 A set of bathroom scales is a type of mass balance

2. Step onto the scales and measure your mass.

3. Record the mass of all the students in your group.

Different types of balance

The choice of **balance** depends on the size and the amount of items to be measured, as well as the accuracy required. All types of balance need to be correctly zeroed when no mass is on them, otherwise you will get an **error**.

When we talk about your 'weight' being, say, 60 kg, we really mean your mass. Kilograms (kg) and grams (g) are units of mass. 'Weighing' something means finding its mass in kilograms. Weight is something different, which you will find out about later.

FIG 2.16 An electronic balance gives an accurate digital readout

FIG 2.17 Other types of mass balance

The instruments in Figs 2.16 and 2.17 measure mass. In everyday language, people talk about measuring the weight of rice or sugar. In fact they are measuring the mass.

Check your understanding

1. Why is it necessary for a balance to be initially positioned at '0'?

2. If you are measuring a very big mass like a suitcase, does the balance need to be very accurate?

3. Why is it important to use a sensitive balance for a very small mass?

Fun fact

A bee hummingbird's mass is less than that of a penny.

Key term

balance instrument used to measure mass

Measuring time

We are learning how to:

- identify appropriate instruments for measuring time
- measure short periods as accurately as possible.

Time »»

Time is what is measured by clocks and watches. It is the period during which events occur.

Activity 2.12

Choosing a time-measuring instrument

Look at the instruments in Fig 2.18. Say which instrument(s) you could you use to measure the time of the following. If more than one is possible, state which instrument would be best, and why.

What would you use to measure:

- The time to boil an egg?
- A professional athlete sprinting a set distance?
- The length of a movie?
- The time to get dressed in the morning?

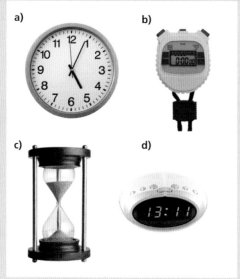

FIG 2.18 Time-measuring instruments:
a) mechanical clock, **b)** stopwatch, **c)** hourglass, **d)** digital clock

FIG 2.19

Time-measuring instruments have been designed to suit both the accuracy and the length of time measurement required. To find the time a professional sprinter takes to run a race, it is important to know the time to within a millisecond.

Activity 2.13

Using a stopwatch

In this activity you will work outdoors in a group.

Here is what you need:

- stopwatch.

Here is what you should do:

1. Decide on a number of walking paces to time.

2. Each member of the group, in turn, should then take the chosen number of paces, while another student measures the time taken using the stopwatch.

3. Record all your results in a table.

4. How did you decide when to start the stopwatch and when to stop it? Comment on the accuracy of your measurements. How could you improve the accuracy?

Activity 2.14

Measuring short periods of time

In this activity you will work in a group. You will measure the period between each of your heartbeats. You can feel your heartbeat as your pulse, for example in your wrist (see Fig 2.20).

Here is what you need:

- stopwatch
- calculator.

Here is what you should do:

1. Use the stopwatch to find the number of pulse beats in one minute for each group member:

   - when sitting down
   - after running around (if you are outside) or jumping up and down on the spot for about a minute.

2. Record all your results in a table.

3. Work out, for each student, the time in seconds between each heartbeat when sitting and after exercising.

4. What is your conclusion?

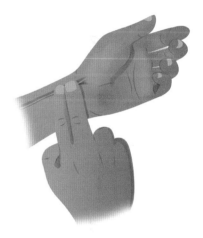

FIG 2.20

> **Fun fact**
>
> A moment, as given by an old English system of time units, is 90 seconds long.

Check your understanding

1. Why was it a good idea to measure the number of pulse beats in one minute and then do a calculation, rather than try to measure the time between each pulse beat?

Measuring temperature

We are learning how to:
- correctly read a thermometer
- describe different types of thermometer.

Temperature ⟩⟩⟩

Temperature is the measure of how hot a body or a substance is. Hotter things have higher temperatures. Colder things have lower temperatures.

Activity 2.15

Reading a thermometer

Here is what you need:
- liquid-in-glass thermometer (be very careful when handling it).

Here is what you should do:

1. Hold the thermometer at the top and observe the reading. Why should you read the scale with your eye level at the top of the liquid column? Why is the temperature reading not zero?

2. Keep your eye on the liquid column and hold the bulb. What happens? Explain your observation.

3. Place the bulb under cold running water. Take the reading and discuss your findings.

FIG 2.21 A liquid-in-glass thermometer

Temperature is a measure of the warmth, or 'hotness', of a substance.

A thermometer measures temperature in degrees Celsius (°C) or sometimes degrees Fahrenheit (°F). In science, the SI unit of temperature (see page 26) is kelvin (K).

A **liquid-in-glass thermometer** contains mercury (a poisonous liquid metal) or coloured alcohol. The liquid expands when heat is applied, so the column of liquid rises up the scale with increasing temperature.

When reading a liquid-in-glass thermometer scale, just as with a measuring cylinder (see Activity 2.7), you must avoid parallax errors to ensure accuracy.

Fun fact

These days the Fahrenheit temperature scale is only used in some weather forecasts. You can convert Fahrenheit temperatures to Celsius by subtracting 32 from the Fahrenheit number, and multiplying by 5/9.

Other types of thermometer

Among the common types of thermometer are digital and liquid-crystal thermometers (Fig 2.22). How does each of these show the temperature?

A digital thermometer (Fig 2.22(a)) consists of an electronic system activated by warmth. A liquid-crystal thermometer (Fig 2.22(b)) contains coloured substances that light up at particular levels of warmth.

Nurses and doctors use liquid-in-glass clinical thermometers. These thermometers cover a small range, because body temperature does not fall below 35 °C or rise above 42 °C. The small range means that the scale can have small divisions and so readings can be more precise.

a)

b)

FIG 2.22 It is important to be able to measure our body temperature: **a)** a clinical thermometer; **b)** a simple thermometer used at home

FIG 2.23 A liquid-in-glass clinical thermometer

Check your understanding

1. Find the reading on the thermometers in Fig 2.25. Give your answers in degrees Celsius.

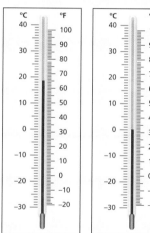
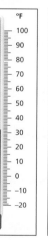
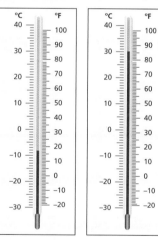

FIG 2.25

FIG 2.24 A medical infra-red thermometer

Fun fact

Infra-red thermometers were used in airports on travellers coming from West Africa during the *Ebola* crisis in 2014 and 2015. These thermometers were able to show quickly anyone who had a fever.

Key terms

temperature a measure of how hot a body is

liquid-in-glass thermometer a device for measuring temperature

Review of Measurement

- Measuring is determining some physical quantity of matter by using instruments marked in standard units.

- Measuring and the use of standard units makes it possible to communicate measurements clearly.

- Estimation provides a useful guide when measuring instruments are not available.

- Length – how long an object is or how long a distance is – is measured in metres (m) or multiples/submultiples of the metre, such as kilometre (km) or centimetre (cm).

- Volume – how much space an object occupies – is measured in cubic cm (cm^3), litres (l) or millilitres (ml).

- Mass – how much matter an object contains – is measured in kilograms (kg) or grams (g).

- Time – how long an event lasts – is measured in seconds (s), minutes (min) or hours (h).

- Temperature – how hot an object is – is measured in kelvin (K), degrees Celsius (°C) or degrees Fahrenheit (°F).

- There is an internationally used set of units, called 'SI units', which includes the metre (m), kilogram (kg), second (s) and kelvin (K).

- Rulers, metre rules, tape measures and callipers are all used to measure distance.

- The volume of a liquid can be found using a measuring cylinder.

- The volume of an irregular solid can be found by the displacement of a liquid.

- A balance is used to measure mass.

- Time-measuring instruments include stopwatches, mechanical clocks and digital clocks.

- Some common thermometers include digital, liquid-crystal and liquid-in-glass thermometers.

- The correct positioning of the eye when reading a scale eliminates parallax errors.

- When measuring the volume of a liquid, the bottom of a concave meniscus or the top of a convex meniscus must be read at eye level.

- In measuring, the chosen instrument must be suitable for what is to be measured as well as for the level of accuracy required.

- Instruments should be correctly set to zero before use if possible, or any zero error accounted for.

Review questions on Measurement

1. What is meant by 'measuring', and why do we measure?
2. a) Identify five important quantities that we measure.
   b) Give the SI unit of each of the quantities in a).
   c) Which instruments are used to measure each?

3. Draw a meniscus that is:

a) concave **b)** convex.

4. Give the reading for the volume of liquid in each of the measuring cylinders shown in Fig 2.26.

a)

b)

c)

d)

FIG 2.26

5. Explain how to find the volume of an irregular solid.

6. A 30 cm³ volume of water was placed in a cylinder, and a stone was dropped in. The water level rose to 35 cm³. Is it true to say that the volume of the stone was 5 cm³?

7. Explain how you would use internal callipers to find the diameter of a cup.

8. Describe how you would find the mass of one red bean using a kitchen scale.

9. How is time defined?

10. How many seconds are in $2\frac{1}{2}$ minutes?

11. A bus left Port of Spain at 1:25 p.m. and arrived in Taco at 4:12 p.m. How long did the journey last?

12. Is 20:25 in the morning or evening? Rewrite the time using a.m. or p.m.

13. Convert 9:23 p.m. into a time using the 24-hour clock.

14. Both an analogue clock and a digital clock have stopped working. How many times will each be correct in one day?

15. What happens in a thermometer so that a temperature can be read?

16. In what units is temperature measured?

17. The news reported that the temperature in New York was –2 °C. By midday, the temperature had risen by 5 °C. What was the temperature at midday?

Unit 3: Characteristics of living things

We are learning how to:

- find out more about living things
- look at how living things are different and how they are similar
- identify features they all have that tell us they are living.

Things can be similar and different

Animals and plants come in different shapes and sizes. Some are very large, while others are so small they can only be seen with the use of a microscope.

Stones also come in different shapes and sizes. Does this mean that stones are living things? What are the features of living things that make them different from non-living things?

FIG 3.1 Living things

FIG 3.2 Non-living things

Seven characteristics are associated with living things:

Growth

Respiration

Irritability

Movement

Nutrition

Excretion

Reproduction

If you take the first letter of each characteristic, it spells GRIMNER. This will help you to remember them.

All living things exhibit all seven characteristics, but some characteristics are easier to observe than others in different organisms.

Living things are made of cells

All living things are composed of cells. Some simple organisms, like *Euglena*, consist of only a single cell. More complex organisms contain many millions of cells.

FIG 3.3 *Euglena*, a unicellular organism

The human body contains many different types of cell. Tissues are composed of many similar cells. The different tissues combine to form organs.

Photosynthesis

FIG 3.4 Green plants carry out photosynthesis

Many of the cells in a green plant contain a pigment called chlorophyll. These cells carry out a process called photosynthesis, which makes food for the plants and also for the animals that eat the plants.

Substances enter and leave cells

In order for organisms to flourish, substances must be able to pass into and out of cells. Substances do this by the processes of diffusion and osmosis.

Key terms

growth the process by which an organism gets bigger

respiration the process by which living things obtain energy

irritability the ability of an organism to respond to a stimulus

movement the ability of an organism to move position or place

nutrition the process by which an organism obtains the food necessary to sustain its life

excretion the removal of waste products from the body of an organism

reproduction the process by which organisms produce offspring

Fun fact

FIG 3.5 Mars explorer *Curiosity*

The explorer *Curiosity* landed on Mars in 2012. *Curiosity* has instruments to examine the rocks and soil. What evidence might it find that there is or has been life on Mars?

Growth

We are learning how to:

- describe the characteristics of living things
- relate growth to living things.

Growth >>>

All living things **grow** in size as they get older. Some organisms grow to their **mature** size very quickly, while others may take many years.

Redwood trees may live and grow for a thousand years. They are the largest and tallest trees in the world.

The appearance of many plants and animals does not change much as they grow. The mature organism often looks to be just a large version of the **young** one.

In some animals, we can see small differences between young and mature forms. For example, a calf looks very similar to a cow but is much smaller, its features are more rounded and it does not have horns.

FIG 3.6 Redwood trees

Activity 3.1

Growing red bean seedlings

Here is what you will need:

- red bean seedlings × 5
- ruler
- water.

Here is what you should do:

1. Label your bean seedlings A, B, C, D and E.

2. Measure the height of each seedling every day for 10 days.

3. Copy and complete Table 3.1 with your results.

FIG 3.7 Cow and calf

Day	1	2	3	4	5	6	7	8	9	10
A										
B										
C										
D										
E										
Average										

TABLE 3.1

4. Calculate the average height of the seedlings each day, by adding all five seedling heights for one day together and dividing the total by 5.

5. Use your data to plot a graph of the average height of the seedlings against time.

Certain groups of animals, including some insects and amphibians, completely change their appearance as they grow. This process is called **metamorphosis**.

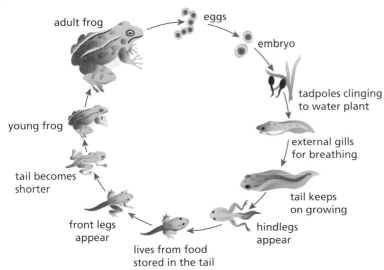

FIG 3.8 Life cycle of a frog

When frogspawn hatches, the eggs develop into tadpoles. The tadpoles have no limbs and they have gills for breathing in water. As the tadpoles grow, they slowly change into adult frogs with four limbs. The gills are replaced by lungs, because the frog spends most of its adult life on land.

Check your understanding

1. Fig 3.9 shows how the average height of boys and girls increases with age.

   a) During which period is the rate of growth greatest?

   b) At what age does a girl reach her maximum height?

   c) At what age does a boy reach his maximum height?

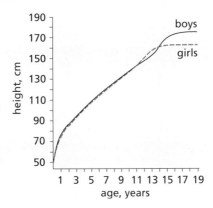

FIG 3.9

Key terms

growth the process by which an organism gets bigger

mature an organism in the latter part of the life cycle when it is fully grown

young an organism in the early part of the life cycle when it is still growing

metamorphosis a process that brings about a complete change in the form of an animal as part of its life cycle

Fun fact

Different parts of the human body grow at different rates, so our shape changes as we grow up. Fig 3.10 shows how the relative sizes of the different parts of the body change as a baby grows into an adult.

FIG 3.10 Shape of the human body at different ages

Respiration

We are learning how to:

- describe the characteristics of living things
- relate respiration to living things.

Respiration »»

Respiration is the process by which cells produce energy. Respiration is not the same as breathing.

All the cells in an organism require energy for the different chemical processes going on inside them. This energy is obtained from the reaction between **glucose** and **oxygen**.

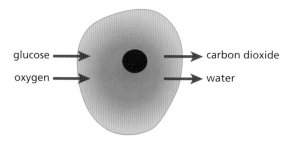

FIG 3.11 Cell respiration

Glucose and oxygen enter the cell, while **carbon dioxide** and **water** – the waste products of respiration – pass in the opposite direction.

The process of cell respiration can be summarised by the following word equation:

glucose + oxygen $\longrightarrow$ carbon dioxide + water + energy

All organisms carry out cell respiration. The way in which an organism obtains the glucose and oxygen it needs and expels the waste products formed depends on its structure.

Many simple unicellular organisms, like amoeba, live in water. Substances can pass into the organism from the water and also out of the organism.

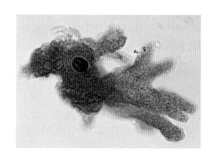

FIG 3.12 An amoeba

FIG 3.13 A banana leaf

Green plants make their own glucose by photosynthesis. Gases pass into and out of a plant through openings in the underside of the leaves.

Complex animals like humans have too many cells for substances to be able to pass directly into the cells from outside the body. Such animals have a circulatory system that carries materials to and from the cells. In humans, glucose and oxygen are carried to the cells in the blood. Waste products are removed from the cells in the same way.

FIG 3.14 Humans have a circulatory system that allows their cells to respire

Check your understanding

1. Copy and complete the following sentences.

   a) Respiration is the process by which living things produce ....

   b) The substances needed for cell respiration are .... and ....

   c) The waste products of cell respiration are .... and ....

Fun fact

The amount of energy a person needs each day depends on two factors, which are their:

- basic metabolic rate
- level of activity.

Basic metabolic rate is the energy needed to keep the body working even when it is resting. This accounts for 60–70% of the body's energy needs.

Key terms

respiration the process by which living things obtain energy

glucose a simple sugar

oxygen a gas found in the air, which is made during photosynthesis and used up during respiration and combustion

carbon dioxide a gas found in the air, which is made during respiration and combustion, and used up during photosynthesis

water a liquid required by all forms of life to survive

Irritability

We are learning how to:

- describe the characteristics of living things
- relate irritability to living things.

Irritability ⟫⟫

Irritability is sometimes also called **sensitivity**. It is the ability of a living thing to react to a **stimulus**. This might be a chemical stimulus such as a harmful chemical, or it might be a physical stimulus such as light.

Microscopic aquatic organisms like algae are attracted to light. The organisms that feed on them, like *Daphnia*, also respond to this stimulus.

Activity 3.2

Measuring the response of worms to light and damp

Here is what you need:

- flat box
- filter paper × 2
- soil
- small worms × 10
- piece of card, at least half the size of the box.

Here is what you should do:

1. Draw pencil lines to divide the flat box into four regions.

2. Sprinkle a thin layer of soil on the bottom of the box. This will help the worms to move about.

3. Place pieces of damp filter paper in opposite corners of the box.

FIG 3.15 *Daphnia* are attracted to the light in search of food

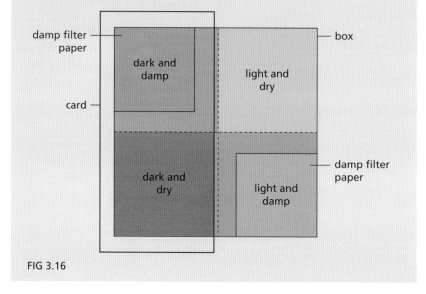

FIG 3.16

Key terms

irritability the ability of an organism to respond to a stimulus

sensitivity an awareness of different stimuli such as light or sound

stimulus a thing or an event that causes an organism to respond in a particular way

response the behaviour of an organism to a stimulus

4. Cover half of the box with a piece of card so that you create four regions where the conditions are different.

5. Place ten small worms in the middle of box and leave the box somewhere quiet for 15 minutes or so.

6. After 15 minutes, count the number of worms in each of the four regions.

7. Consider how worms react to the stimuli of light and damp.

8. Release the worms back into the wild unharmed.

Animals respond to stimuli in different ways. A stimulus might attract some animals while having the opposite effect on others. For example, woodlice prefer a dark environment, so they will respond to light in an appropriate way.

FIG 3.17 Plant stems grow towards the light

The **response** of plants to stimuli such as light is much less obvious that the response of animals, because it takes much longer. If a plant is placed on a windowsill, its stem will grow towards the light over a few days.

The human body has sense organs that respond to a number of different stimuli.

Check your understanding

1. Copy and complete Table 3.2 with the sense organ that responds to each of the stimuli given.

Stimulus	Sense organ
touch	
sound	
taste	
light	
smell	

TABLE 3.2

Fun fact

FIG 3.18 **a)** Charaille and **b)** 'sensitive plant'

Some plants respond to touch. Charaille (*Momordica charantia*) has hairy tendrils that sense touch and can move away from an object touching them. The 'sensitive plant' (*Mimosa pudica*) has leaves that curl up when touched.

Movement

We are learning how to:

- describe the characteristics of living things
- relate movement to living things.

Movement >>>

All organisms are able to **move**, although animals move much more freely than plants. Plants move their parts while staying in a fixed position.

The way in which animals move depends on their body structure.

Birds are able to move through the air because their upper limbs have evolved into **wings**. They also have other features, like hollow bones, that help them to fly.

FIG 3.19 Birds can fly because they have wings

FIG 3.20 Some land animals move about on legs

Many land animals move about on two, four or more **legs**.

Animals like snakes are able to move about on land and in water without the help of legs. They push themselves along by contractions of their muscular bodies.

FIG 3.21 Some land animals are able to move without legs

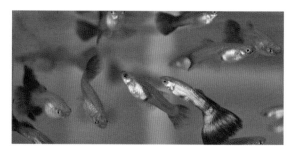

FIG 3.22 Fish are ideally shaped to move through water

Fish have muscular bodies that can propel them through the water. They have evolved without limbs, which would spoil their streamlined shape and slow them down.

FIG 3.23 Mangroves can alter the directions in which their leaves point

Although plants cannot change their position, they can turn their leaves either towards the Sun, in order to get the most light, or away from the Sun to protect them from burning during the hottest part of the day.

Check your understanding

1. Penguins are birds but they cannot fly. Instead, they spend a lot of time feeding on fish in the water.

FIG 3.24

Look carefully at Fig 3.24 and describe three features that help the penguin to move easily through water.

Fun fact

The millipede *Illacme plenipes* grows to only about 3 cm long but it has up to 750 legs, the most legs of any known animal.

This millipede was first observed in 1926. It was thought to be extinct, but a small colony was discovered in California, USA, in 2005.

Key terms

movement the ability of an organism to move position or place

wings structures that some animals have, which enable them to fly

legs structures that some animals have, which enable them to move about on the ground

Nutrition

We are learning how to:

- describe the characteristics of living things
- relate nutrition to living things.

Nutrition ⟩⟩⟩

Nutrition is about obtaining food. Food is needed for producing energy and for growth. Plants and animals have completely different ways of obtaining their food.

FIG 3.25 Plants make their own food

Plants make their own food by a process called **photosynthesis**. In this process, simple substances are built into complex substances. Energy from sunlight is used to convert carbon dioxide and water into glucose, as shown in the word equation below:

carbon dioxide + water + energy ⟶ glucose + oxygen

You will learn more about photosynthesis later in the book.

All animals depend either directly or indirectly on green plants for their food. Animals obtain their food by eating plants or by eating animals that eat plants.

Animals can be placed in groups according to whether they eat only plants, only other animals or a mixture of plants and animals.

Herbivores eat only plants. Cattle and goats are examples of herbivores. The mouths of herbivores have few or no front teeth, but they have large back teeth so they can grind the plant material before swallowing it. Insects like grasshoppers are also herbivores. They eat the foliage of plants.

FIG 3.26 Goats are herbivores

FIG 3.27 Grasshoppers are herbivores

FIG 3.28 Mongooses are carnivores

FIG 3.29 Praying mantises are carnivores

FIG 3.30 Vultures eat the bodies of dead animals

Carnivores eat only other animals. In order to kill other animals, carnivores like the mongoose have sharp front teeth that can pierce and cut into flesh. Some insects are carnivores. The praying mantis eats other insects.

Scavengers like vultures are another group of carnivores. They do not actually kill other animals but feed off the bodies of animals that are already dead.

FIG 3.31 Quenks are omnivores

Omnivores are animals that eat both plants and other animals. Quenks are omnivores. They eat fruits, seeds and roots but they will also eat small animals like worms and insects.

After animals have eaten, complex substances are broken down into simple substances.

Fun fact

Most people are omnivores. They have a diet of foods obtained both from plants and from animals, although they may not eat meat at every meal. Some people are herbivores. They eat foods obtained from plants but will not eat foods obtained from animals. These people are called vegetarians.

Check your understanding

1. Table 3.3 lists what some different animals eat. Decide whether each animal is a herbivore, a carnivore or an omnivore.

Name of animal	What the animal eats
red brocket deer	plant material
crab-eating racoon	insects, crabs, fruit and berries
owl	small rodents like rats
ghost bat	insects
spiny pocket mouse	seeds
red howler monkey	fruit and insects

TABLE 3.3

Key terms

nutrition the process by which an organism obtains the food necessary to sustain its life

photosynthesis the process in plants by which carbon dioxide and water are converted to glucose using energy from sunlight

herbivore an animal that eats only plants

carnivore an animal that eats only other animals

omnivore an animal that eats both plants and other animals

Excretion

We are learning how to:

- describe the characteristics of living things
- relate excretion to living things.

Excretion »»

Metabolism is a collective word to describe all the chemical processes that occur within a living organism in order to maintain life. Many of these processes produce waste products that are harmful to the organism and must be removed. **Excretion** is the removal of these waste products.

In simple unicellular organisms that live in water, like *Paramecium*, waste products are able to pass directly out of the organism into the surrounding water.

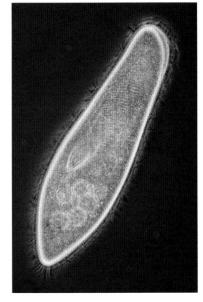

FIG 3.32 *Paramecium*

Activity 3.3

Waste products of yeast metabolism

Here is what you need:

- dried yeast
- test tubes × 2
- rubber bung
- limewater
- teaspoon
- sugar
- test-tube stand
- glass tubing
- distilled water.

Here is what you should do:

1. Place half a teaspoon of dried yeast and half a teaspoon of sugar in the bottom of a test tube.

2. Add water until the test tube is about one-third full.

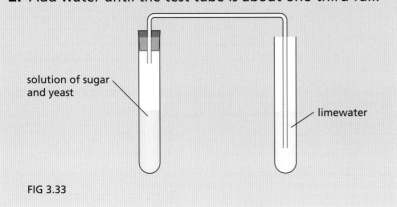

solution of sugar and yeast

limewater

FIG 3.33

3. Half fill a second test tube with limewater.

4. Connect the test tubes with glass tubing as shown in Fig 3.33.

5. Leave the apparatus to stand for a day or until bubbles of gas from the solution of sugar and yeast start to pass through the limewater.

6. How does the appearance of the limewater change?

7. Which gas is a waste product of yeast metabolism?

8. Carefully remove the bung from the test tube containing the solution of sugar and yeast. Smell the contents of the tube. Can you identify another waste product of yeast metabolism?

Some of the carbon dioxide and water produced by green plants as a result of cell respiration is used in photosynthesis. Remaining unwanted gases are able to pass out through tiny pores in the underside of leaves.

Plant metabolism also creates other waste products that are not gases. These are removed from the plant as resin or sap that passes out through the plant stem.

Complex organisms like humans have an excretory system that removes and expels waste products. Carbon dioxide and water are expelled from the body each time we breathe out. Other waste products are removed from the blood by the kidneys and lost from the body in solution as urine.

Excretion should not be confused with the removal of undigested food from the body as faeces. This process is not excretion, because the faeces are not the waste products of metabolic processes; it is called **egestion**.

FIG 3.34 Plant resin

> **Fun fact**
>
> Plants excrete some waste materials in their leaves. The materials are removed when the old leaves fall off the tree to be replaced by new leaves.

Check your understanding

1. Mangroves grow in soil that contains a high level of salt. In order for metabolic processes to take place, the mangrove must remove some of the salt it absorbs. The salt is lost in solution through pores in the underside of the leaves. When the water evaporates, salt crystals may be formed.

FIG 3.35

Is this an example of excretion? Explain your answer.

Key terms

metabolism the chemical processes that take place within an organism in order to maintain life

excretion removal of waste products from the body of an organism

egestion the expulsion of undigested food from the body

Reproduction

We are learning how to:

- describe the characteristics of living things
- relate reproduction to living things.

Reproduction ▶▶▶

All living things reproduce, otherwise organisms would become extinct very quickly. They need to make more individuals of the same kind. However, there is a great variety in the frequency of **reproduction** and the mechanisms by which organisms reproduce. Some organisms reproduce sexually and some reproduce asexually.

Sexual reproduction

Sexual reproduction involves two 'parent' organisms. Flowering plants are able to carry out sexual reproduction. The flower is the reproductive organ.

A hibiscus flower has both **male** parts and **female** parts. During sexual reproduction, the male sex cells, or pollen, are transferred from one flower to the female parts of another flower. This process is called **pollination** and is carried out by insects. The pollen then combines with female sex cells to eventually produce seeds.

Sexual reproduction is the way in which many animals reproduce. In some animals, like birds, the young develop outside the body of the parents. In other animals, like humans, the young develop inside the body of the female.

FIG 3.36 Hibiscus flower

FIG 3.37 In some animals the male and the female look similar, but in others they look different

Fun fact

Slugs, snails and earthworms have both male and female reproductive organs.

FIG 3.38 Earthworms are hermaphrodites

Animals that have both male and female sex organs are called hermaphrodites.

Asexual reproduction

Single-celled organisms are able to reproduce by a process called **binary fission**. Initially, the nucleus divides and then the cytoplasm around it divides. The result is two new cells.

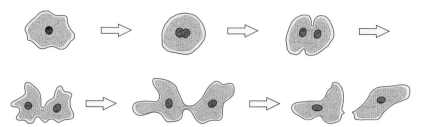

FIG 3.39 Binary fission

Binary fission is also the process by which complex organisms like humans produce new cells for growth and repair.

In **binary fission**, only one 'parent' organism is involved, therefore it is an example of **asexual reproduction**.

Plants are able to undergo asexual reproduction (sometimes also called **vegetative reproduction**) in a number of ways.

New banana plants grow from suckers that develop on the root of a single banana plant. Once the sucker is big enough, it can be separated from the parent plant and will grow on its own.

Members of the *Bryophyllum* group of plants are able to grow new plantlets at the ends of their leaves. These plantlets eventually fall off and start to grow in the ground.

FIG 3.40 A banana sucker

FIG 3.41 Air plant, also known as life plant or miracle leaf

Key terms

reproduction the process by which organisms produce offspring

male the sex that produces sperm (animal) or pollen (plant)

female the sex that produces ovum (animal) or ovule (plant)

pollination the transfer of pollen from one flower to another, either on the same plant or a different plant

binary fission the process by which a cell divides into two equal parts

asexual reproduction a method of reproduction that involves only one parent

vegetative reproduction asexual reproduction in plants

Check your understanding

1. Strawberry plants can reproduce by sending out runners. At the end of each runner a new plant forms.

FIG 3.42

   a) Is this an example of asexual or sexual reproduction?
   b) Explain your answer to a).
   c) What name is sometimes given to this process when it occurs in plants?

Unit 4: What are cells?

We are learning how to:

- compare plant and animal cells according to their structure and function
- describe cells.

What are cells? ▶▶▶

If you look carefully at Fig 4.1 you will see that, although the building is very large, it is built of many individual stones or bricks. If you imagine that an organism is like a building, then, just as the building is composed of stones or bricks, so the organism is composed of **cells**.

The cell is the building block from which all organisms are composed. All plants and animals contain large numbers of cells. Scientists estimate that the human body contains many millions of cells.

A cell is very tiny and cannot be seen with the unaided eye. In order to see a cell, we need a **microscope**. You will have an opportunity to prepare slides and look at cells using a microscope in later lessons.

All cells have certain common features. There are some differences between animal cells and plant cells. You will learn about the differences later in the course. For now we will look at some different examples of each type of cell.

FIG 4.1 Killarney mansion on Queen's Park Savannah, Port of Spain

Animal cells

Animals are composed of cells. Look carefully at these different examples of animal cells.

Although these are all animal cells, they have different shapes and appearances because they have different jobs to do in the body. For example:

- Cheek cells protect the inside of the cheek.

- Red blood cells travel through the blood, carrying oxygen to all the other cells of the body.

- Nerve cells carry nerve impulses.

a)
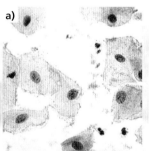

b)
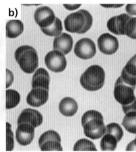

c)
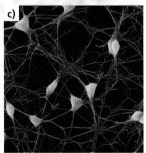

FIG 4.2 Different animal cells:
a) cheek cells,
b) red blood cells and
c) nerve cells

Plant cells

Plants are also composed of cells. Look carefully at the following pictures of cells in a plant.

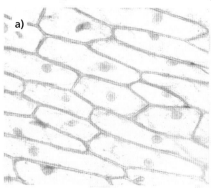 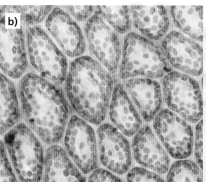 

FIG 4.3 Different plant cells, from **a)** onion epidermis, **b)** leaf and **c)** stem

Once again, we can see a difference in the shape and form of the different cells.

- Epidermal cells are rectangular and fit together to protect the fleshy leaf.

- Leaf cells contain chlorophyll, which captures energy from sunlight. Green plants use this energy in the process of photosynthesis, by which they make food.

- Stem cells are closely packed to provide the plant with support.

Check your understanding

1. Fig 4.5 shows the great Khufu pyramid at Giza in Egypt.

FIG 4.5 The great Khufu pyramid at Giza

a) From what is the pyramid made?

b) How is the structure of the pyramid similar to that of a plant or an animal?

Fun fact

Australian scientists have discovered fossils in rocks that tell us that cells emerged on Earth at least 3.4 billion years ago.

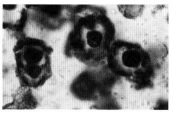

FIG 4.4 Fossil evidence of cells

Key terms

cell the building block from which all living things are made

microscope an optical device that magnifies an image of a specimen, so more detail can be seen

Using a microscope

We are learning how to:

- compare plant and animal cells according to their structure and function
- use a microscope.

Using a microscope ⟫⟫

A **microscope** is an instrument that makes objects look bigger than they really are.

A simple microscope has two lenses, called the **objective lens** and the **eye lens** or eyepiece. These two lenses are fixed at each end of a tube. The tube can be moved up and down in order to focus on an object.

The power, or magnification, of a lens is usually given as a number. For example, an eye lens might typically have a magnification of times 10, or ×10. An objective lens might have a magnification of times 4, or ×4.

The overall magnification of a microscope is the product of the magnification of the two lenses. In the example above, the overall magnification of the microscope is 10 × 4 = ×40. This means that everything you see under the microscope appears 40 times bigger than it actually is.

More sophisticated microscopes have three or four objective lenses of different powers on a rotating turret. A low-power lens can be used to locate the area of a specimen to be examined, and then the high-power lens is used to see that part of the specimen in more detail.

Microscope slides and cover slips

Microscope **slides** are rectangles of glass. The normal size is 75 mm by 25 mm and about 1 mm thick. Microscope slides may be flat or have a small cavity ground into the surface.

eye lens
tube
knob for adjusting focus
rotating turret
objective lenses
stage, where object to be viewed is placed
mirror to shine light on object

FIG 4.6 A microscope with three different objective lenses

Fun fact

Around 1590, two Dutch spectacle makers, Hans and Zacharias Janssen, started experimenting by putting several lenses into tubes. They discovered that looking at an object through the tube made it appear much larger than when looked at with a single magnifying glass.

The Janssens' work was taken up by another Dutchman, called Antonie van Leeuwenhoek. Van Leeuwenhoek made a working microscope that allowed him to see things that no person had ever seen before, like bacteria, blood cells and tiny organisms in droplets of pond water.

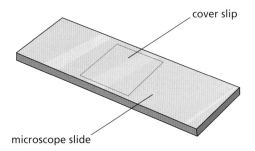
cover slip
microscope slide

FIG 4.7 A microscope slide and cover slip

A specimen is placed on a microscope slide and covered by a much thinner piece of glass called a **cover slip**. The cover slip prevents the specimen from drying out and also protects the objective lens of the microscope.

Activity 4.1

Learning how to use a microscope

Microscopes are expensive to buy and to repair if they are damaged. In this activity you will have the opportunity to learn how to use a microscope correctly.

Here is what you need:

- microscope
- microscope slide.

Here is what you should do:

1. Look at the microscope and identify the parts.

2. Turn the knob that adjusts the focus, and observe how this moves the tube up and down.

3. Put a small specimen in the middle of the microscope slide. For example, you might want to look at a hair.

4. Adjust the microscope until the object comes into focus.

5. If your microscope has more than one objective lens, look at the object using first the low power lens and then the high power lens.

6. Practise drawing what you can see.

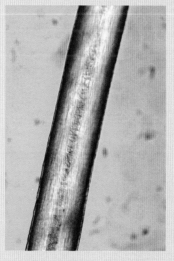

FIG 4.8 A human hair as seen under a microscope magnified 25 times

Key terms

microscope an optical device that magnifies an image of a specimen, so more detail can be seen

objective lens the lens on a microscope that is nearer to the specimen being observed

eye lens the lens on a microscope that is nearer to the eye

slide a small oblong piece of glass upon which a specimen to be examined under a microscope is placed

cover slip a thin disc or square of glass placed on top of a specimen to be viewed under a microscope

Check your understanding

1. A microscope has an eyepiece of power ×10 and three objective lenses of power ×4, ×10 and ×40.

   a) What is the lowest power at which you could look at a specimen with this microscope?

   b) What is the highest power at which you could look at a specimen with this microscope?

Observing a specimen of animal cells

We are learning how to:

- compare plant and animal cells according to their structure and function
- prepare animal cells to view with a microscope.

Different types of animal cells ⟫

There are many different kinds of animal cell. We are going to look at four examples, and observe slides of animal cells under a microscope.

Cheek cells

Cheek cells are obtained by gently scraping the inside of the cheek.

Cells prepared for examination under a microscope are often stained with a dye so the structure can be seen more clearly. **Cheek cells** are stained with **methylene blue**. This makes the cells look blue when examined.

Key terms

cheek cell cells from the inside of the cheek in the mouth

methylene blue a dye that stains materials blue

skeletal muscle cells long, thin cells from the large muscles of the body that can move

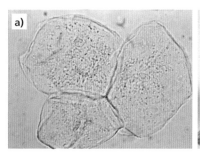 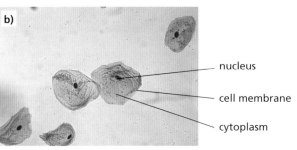

a) b)

nucleus

cell membrane

cytoplasm

FIG 4.9 Cheek cells: **a)** not stained and **b)** stained

It is possible to see the nucleus, cytoplasm and cell membrane of cheek cells after staining.

Muscle cells

There are different types of **muscle cells** in the body. The muscles we use to move our arms and legs are called skeletal muscle.

The muscle cells are long and thin. Do they remind you of the structure of meat? If a person chooses to eat meat, this meat will be mostly animal muscle.

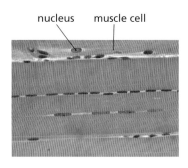

nucleus   muscle cell

FIG 4.10 Skeletal muscle cells

Liver cells

The liver has many important functions in the body. **Liver cells** are much rounder than muscle cells.

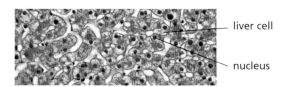

liver cell

nucleus

FIG 4.11 Liver cells

Blood cells

Blood consists of a mixture of particles, including **blood cells,** suspended in a watery liquid called plasma.

There are white blood cells and red blood cells. You will learn more about their different functions later in the course.

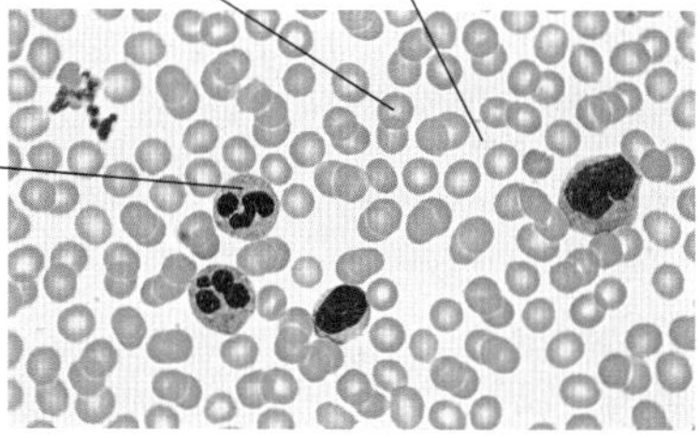

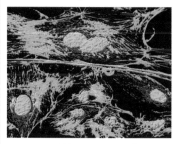

FIG 4.12 Blood cells

red blood cell
plasma
white blood cell

Activity 4.2

Observing prepared slides of animal cells

Here is what you need:

- microscope
- prepared slides of animal cells.

Here is what you should do:

1. Place the first prepared slide under the microscope.

2. Start by observing it under low power. This makes it much easier to see the arrangement of cells, and you can identify particular groups of cells that you would like to see in greater detail.

3. When you have identified a part of your specimen that you would like to see in greater detail, move the slide so that this part is in the centre of the image.

4. Change the combination of the eyepiece and objective lenses to see the image under higher power.

5. Draw the cells and label any parts you recognise.

6. Repeat this for the other prepared slides.

Fun fact

Cells are sometimes stained with combinations of different dyes.

FIG 4.13 Different parts of a cell show up in different colours

Each dye is absorbed by a different part of the cell, so the parts are easier to see.

Check your understanding

1. Fig 4.14 shows some skin cells.

   Draw a single skin cell and label the nucleus, cytoplasm and cell membrane.

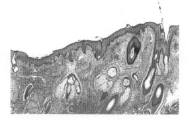

FIG 4.14 Skin cells

Key terms

liver cells cells from the liver that are round and carry out many functions

blood cells cells from the blood; some are red and carry gases, others are white and fight infections

Structure of an animal cell

We are learning how to:

- compare plant and animal cells according to their structure and function
- identify parts of an animal cell.

Structure of an animal cell ≫

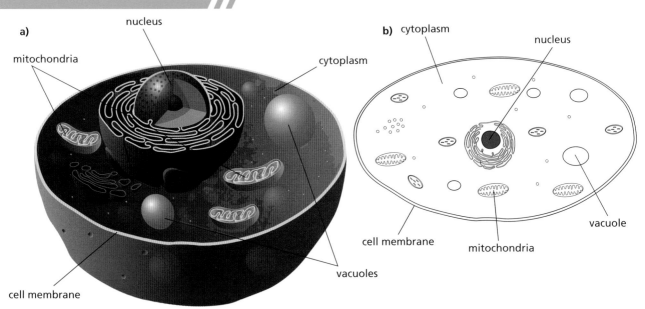

FIG 4.15 Structure of an animal cell: **a)** in three dimensions; **b)** as a scientific drawing

Fig 4.15 shows the structure of a typical animal cell. The cell has three main parts.

1. The **nucleus** is a small dark structure inside the cell. It contains **chromosomes**.

2. The **cytoplasm** is a jelly-like substance that fills the cell. It contains these important structures:

   - **mitochondria** (singular mitochondrion)
   - **glycogen grains**
   - small **vacuoles**.

3. The **cell membrane** is a thin layer that surrounds the cell.

Nucleus

The nucleus controls and coordinates all the processes, such as respiration, that take place within the cell. If you imagine a cell to be like a computer, then the nucleus is the central processor. The nucleus was the first part of a cell to be discovered by scientists.

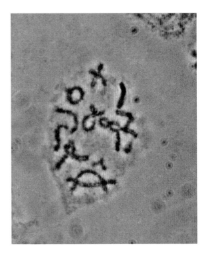

FIG 4.16 Chromosomes are found in the nucleus of a cell

Chromosomes, which are found in the nucleus, are important because they contain all the information the cell needs to function and to replicate itself – the genetic information.

Cytoplasm

The cytoplasm is where many complex chemical reactions take place in the cell. Cytoplasm has a number of important components, including the following:

- **Mitochondria** – These are sometimes described as the cell's power plant, because they provide the cell with energy.
- **Glycogen grains** – All cells need glucose to carry out cell respiration. Glucose is stored inside cells in the form of another chemical, called glycogen. When the cell needs energy, glycogen molecules can be quickly converted back into glucose.
- **Small vacuoles** – Small vacuoles are often found in animal cells. They are bubbles filled with water containing dissolved substances.

Cell membrane

The cell membrane surrounds the cell. It has an important function in controlling the movement of materials into and out of the cell.

Check your understanding

1. Fig 4.17 represents an animal cell.

a) What are the parts labelled X, Y and Z?

b) Which of the labelled parts:

i) contains mitochondria?

ii) controls the activity of the cell?

iii) controls the movement of substances into and out of the cell?

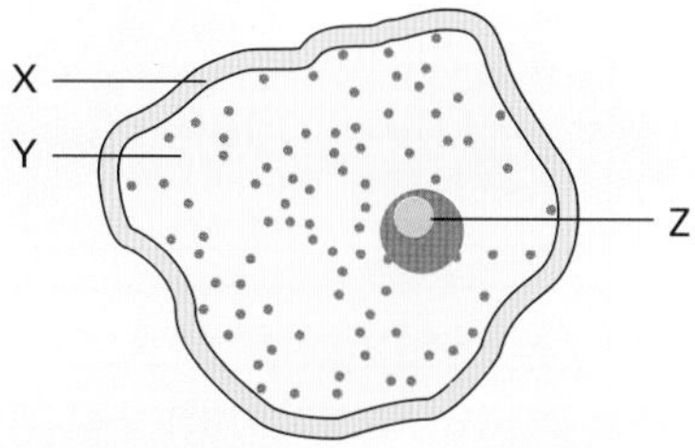

FIG 4.17

Fun fact

Cells were first observed by Robert Hooke in 1665 using a crude microscope of low magnification. One observation was from very thin slices of cork. He saw many tiny pores that we now know are filled with air. Hooke did not know what the pores were, but called them 'cells', from the Latin word *cella*, which means a small room like the ones where monks lived.

Key terms

nucleus the part of a cell that controls the processes that take place in it

chromosomes structures in the nucleus that carry information which allows the cell to duplicate itself

cytoplasm a jelly-like substance that surrounds the nucleus in a cell

mitochondria structures in the cytoplasm responsible for the release of energy

glycogen grains the means by which glucose is stored in animal cells

vacuole a space within a cell containing fluid

cell membrane a membrane that surrounds the cell and controls what enters and leaves it

Preparing a specimen of plant cells

We are learning how to:

- compare plant and animal cells according to their structure and function
- prepare plant cells to view with a microscope.

Preparing a specimen of plant cells ⟫

Although there are many different kinds of plant cell, a convenient source of cells is the thin membrane of **epidermal cells** between the layers of an onion. This membrane is only one cell thick.

Onion cells are normally stained with **iodine solution** to make them easier to observe.

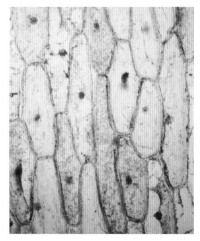

FIG 4.18 Epidermal cells in the membrane between the layers of an onion

Activity 4.3

Preparing and observing onion cells

Here is what you need:

- microscope
- cover slip
- piece of onion
- scalpel
- scissors
- microscope slide
- iodine solution
- tissue paper
- tweezers
- distilled water.

Here is what you should do:

1. Peel part of a layer from an onion. If you look carefully at the inside of the piece you have removed, you will see a thin membrane. This is duller in appearance than the outside of the onion.

2. Using a scalpel or small knife, very carefully start to separate the membrane from the onion, and then remove it completely using a pair of tweezers.

3. The piece of material you remove is likely to be far bigger than will sensibly fit on a microscope slide. Using scissors, cut off a piece of the membrane, about 5 mm by 5 mm, and place it on a clean slide.

4. Add a drop of distilled water to make a wet mount.

5. Add a single drop of iodine solution to the distilled water and leave it for 1 minute.

FIG 4.19 Peeling an onion

6. Lower a cover slip onto the specimen so that it is sitting on the surface of the water.

7. Using a tissue as a wick, remove the excess water and iodine solution from under the cover slip. The tissue might discolour when it comes into contact with the iodine.

8. Ensure your slide is dry before placing it on the microscope. Wipe the top and bottom of the slide with a clean tissue. Take care not to move the specimen and cover slip.

9. Onion cells are significantly larger than cheek cells, so you will not need such high magnification to see them in detail. Set your microscope to the lowest power available and look at your specimen.

10. Find an area of your specimen where the onion cells have stained well and you can see lots of detail. Make this the centre of your field of view and change your microscope to a higher power.

11. Draw your onion cells.

Onion cells are regular in shape. They are rectangular and fit together like bricks in a wall. Onion cells have both thin cell membranes and thick cell walls, so the outline of the cell is easy to see.

Although onion cells are plant cells, they do not have chloroplasts. Chloroplasts contain the green pigment chlorophyll. The plant uses chlorophyll during photosynthesis to make food (glucose).

Check your understanding

1. **a)** Explain why specimens to be viewed with a microscope are stained with a dye.

   b) Suggest a suitable dye with which to stain onion skin cells.

2. Fig 4.21 shows onion cells seen through a microscope. The eyepiece used was ×10 and the objective lens ×4. The distance across the picture is 32 mm.

   a) What was the overall magnification of the microscope?

   b) Estimate the length of an onion cell in millimetres (mm).

4.5

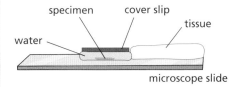

specimen   cover slip

tissue

water

microscope slide

FIG 4.20

Fun fact

An onion plant has both leaves and a bulb. The leaves are green because they contain chlorophyll. Here food is made. The onion is a bulb and is the part of the plant designed to store food and not make it. Since the onion bulb does not make food, the cells do not need chlorophyll.

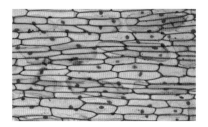

FIG 4.21 Onion cells

Key terms

epidermal cells cells that come from the epidermis, or skin, between layers of an onion

iodine solution a substance that forms a distinctive blue-black colour when mixed with starch

Structure of plant cells

We are learning how to:

- compare plant and animal cells according to their structure and function
- identify parts of a plant cell.

Structure of plant cells ≫

If you look carefully at the structure of a typical plant cell shown in Fig 4.22, you will see that it has some parts that are found in animal cells and also some extra parts that are not.

Plant cells contain a nucleus, chromosomes, cytoplasm, mitochondria and a cell membrane. There are also some important additional features.

1. Plant cells generally have much larger vacuoles than animal cells do.

2. All plant cells are surrounded by a **cell wall** made of cellulose.

3. Many plant cells have chloroplasts. Inside the **chloroplasts** is a green pigment called chlorophyll. This pigment is responsible for the colour of the leaves and stems of plants.

4. Plant cells contain **starch grains**.

Cell wall

A plant cell has both a cell membrane and, surrounding it, a cell wall. Cell walls are made of cellulose. The cell wall around a plant cell has a different role from the cell membrane. Tough and rigid, but also with some flexibility, the cell wall provides a plant cell with structural support while protecting it.

The cell wall also prevents the plant cell from over-expanding when it absorbs water. Together, the rigid cell wall and the pressure of water in the cells allow a plant stem to stand upright.

Chloroplasts

Chloroplasts are the most obvious feature of a plant cell. The word 'chloroplast' comes from the Greek words meaning 'green thing'. Green is the colour we associate with all plants.

The role of chloroplasts is to trap energy from sunlight during photosynthesis. Each chloroplast contains a pigment called chlorophyll, which is responsible for the characteristic green colour.

a)

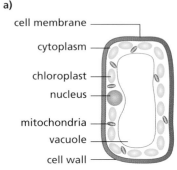

cell membrane
cytoplasm
chloroplast
nucleus
mitochondria
vacuole
cell wall

b)

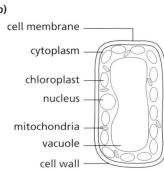

cell membrane
cytoplasm
chloroplast
nucleus
mitochondria
vacuole
cell wall

FIG 4.22 Structure of a plant cell: **a)** in three dimensions; **b)** as a scientific diagram

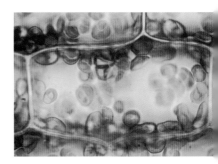

FIG 4.23 Chloroplasts in plant cells

Vacuoles

Vacuoles are present in many animal cells, but they are generally much larger in plant cells. Vacuoles are filled with an aqueous solution containing different chemical compounds.

The role of vacuoles varies greatly according to the type of cell. In plant cells, the role of the large vacuole includes:

- isolating substances that might be harmful
- containing waste products
- transferring unwanted substances from the cell
- maintaining turgor pressure within the cell, which allows the plant to support structures like leaves and flowers.

Starch grains

Glucose is not present in plant cells as glycogen but as starch. Starch is another example of a storage polymer.

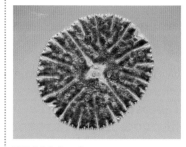
Activity 4.4

Modelling a plant cell

Here is what you will need:

- modelling clay – several different colours
- modelling tools to flatten and cut the clay
- toothpicks
- small labels.

Here is what you should do:

1. Build a model of a plant cell using modelling clay.
2. Your model should have all the parts that you would expect to see in a plant cell. Each part should be a different colour.
3. When you have completed your model, write a label for each part. Attach each label to one end of a toothpick and place the other end in the part.

Key terms

cell wall the outer layer of a plant cell

chloroplast a structure in a plant cell that contains the green pigment chlorophyll, which traps the energy needed for photosynthesis

starch grain the means by which glucose is stored in plant cells

Check your understanding

1. Fig 4.25 shows the structure of a plant root cell.

   a) Name parts A, B, C and D.
   b) What structure found in a leaf cell would you not expect to find in a root cell?
   c) Explain your answer to b).

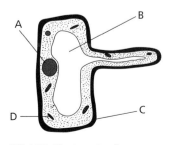

FIG 4.25 Plant root cell

Unit 5: Cells, tissues and organs

We are learning how to:

- recognise the relationships between specialised cells, tissues, organs and organ systems
- describe cells, tissues and organs.

Cells, tissues and organs ❯❯

Cells are the building blocks from which all **organisms** are formed. Some simple organisms, like yeast and amoeba, are described as unicellular because they are composed of a single cell. More complex organisms, like humans and flowering plants, are described as multicellular because they are composed of many cells.

These cells are arranged in **tissues**, the tissues form parts of an **organ**, and the organ forms part of an organ **system**.

cells → tissues → organs → systems → organism

Fig 5.1 shows the relationship between cells, tissues and organs in the human digestive system.

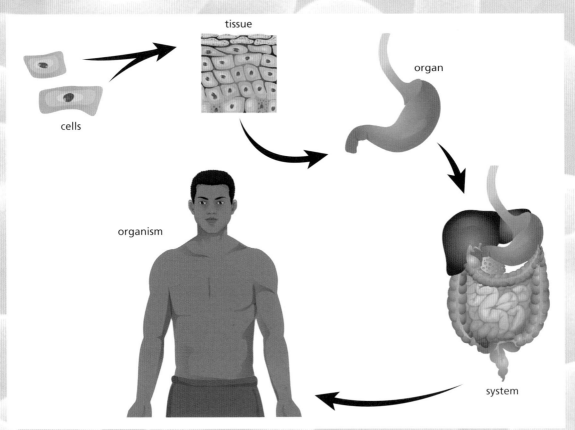

FIG 5.1 The human digestive system

The human digestive system contains different types of cells. The cells are grouped together to form different types of tissue.

The stomach is an organ of the digestive system. It is composed of different types of tissue. The small intestine is another organ of the digestive system. It is also composed of tissue, but the tissue is different from that of the stomach.

The stomach, small intestine and other organs together are called the digestive system.

The digestive system is one of a number of different organ systems in the human body.

The transport system of a plant moves water and nutrients from one part to another. It contains different types of cells grouped to form different types of tissue. The root is an organ of the transport system.

The transport system is one of a number of different organ systems in a plant.

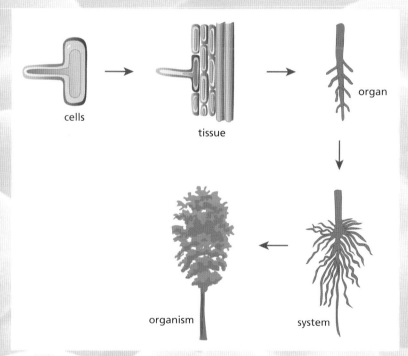

FIG 5.2 The transport system of a plant

Key terms

cell the building block from which all living things are made

organism a living thing

tissue a collection of cells that are similar in structure

organ a part of an organism that is self-contained and has a particular function

system a collection of two or more organs that have related functions

Check your understanding

1. Arrange the following in order, starting with the simplest:

    system   tissue   cell   organism   tissue

Unicellular organisms

We are learning how to:

- recognise the relationships between specialised cells, tissues, organs and organ systems
- identify unicellular organisms.

Multicellular and unicellular organisms

Living organisms like human beings are described as **multicellular** because they consist of many millions of cells. Some very simple organisms consist of only one cell and are called **unicellular**. A unicellular organism carries out all of the activities of a living thing.

You have already seen one unicellular organism, *Euglena*, on page 47. We are going to look at some more examples.

Amoeba

An **amoeba** is a microscopic unicellular organism that lives in ponds and streams.

It has all of the characteristics of a living organism (see Section 3.1). An amoeba can:

- carry out respiration to obtain energy
- absorb nutrients through its cell membrane
- excrete waste products through its cell membrane
- grow bigger
- reproduce by dividing into two new organisms
- move by allowing its cytoplasm to flow
- respond to stimuli, such as chemicals dissolved in water.

Paramecium

A *Paramecium* is another microscopic unicellular organism that lives in water.

It also exhibits all of the seven characteristics of a living organism. It is able to move more quickly than an amoeba because it is covered in tiny hair-like cilia that can beat together and propel it through the water.

Yeast

Yeast is a unicellular fungus. It has been used by people since ancient times to make bread and also to make alcoholic drinks by a process called fermentation.

Key terms

multicellular describes an organism that consists of many cells

unicellular describes an organism that consists of a single cell

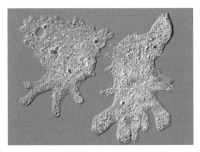

FIG 5.3 An amoeba is a unicellular organism

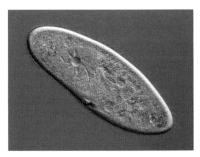

FIG 5.4 A *Paramecium* is a unicellular organism

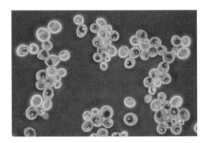

FIG 5.5 Every cell of yeast is a unicellular organism

Yeast reproduce by a process called **budding**. New cells grow from existing cells. If you look carefully at Fig 5.5 you will see that some of the yeast cells appear to be growing tiny buds. Each new small cell grows and then separates from its parent cell.

Activity 5.1

Observing yeast cells

Here is what you need:

- microscope
- microscope slide
- cover slip
- tissue paper
- pipette
- bottle of solution containing yeast cells.

Here is what you should do:

1. Shake the solution of yeast cells and remove a small amount in a pipette.

2. Place two drops of the yeast solution onto a microscope slide.

3. Carefully lower a cover slip onto the specimen.

4. Place a tissue next to the cover slip and gently draw off the excess water.

5. Place the slide on the stage of the microscope.

6. Observe the yeast cells using a low magnification. Look for yeast cells that appear to be budding, then examine these cells using a higher magnification.

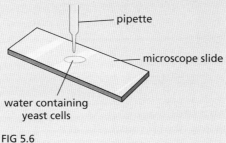

7. Draw some budding yeast cells.

FIG 5.6

Check your understanding

1. Fig 5.7 shows an organism called *Nassula*.

   a) Is *Nassula* better described as a unicellular organism or a multicellular organism?

   b) What characteristics of living organisms would you expect *Nassula* to have?

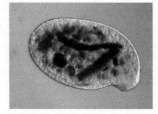

FIG 5.7 *Nassula*

Fun fact

At one time, the living world was classified by scientists into two kingdoms: plants and animals. Unicellular organisms were classified as either animals or plants, depending on which they most closely resembled. The amoeba was considered to be an animal while *Euglena* was considered to be a plant.

Eventually, scientists realised that unicellular organisms did not really fit either of these kingdoms. The classification of the living world was revised to give the five kingdoms we have today. Unicellular organisms now have their own kingdom, called Protista.

Key terms

An amoeba a tiny single-celled (unicellular) organism

Paramecium a tiny single-celled organism with small hairs on its surface

yeast a single-celled fungus which brings about fermentation

budding a system of reproduction where young cells bud off from the parent cell

Respiratory system

We are learning how to:

- recognise the relationships between specialised cells, tissues, organs and organ systems
- identify parts of the respiratory system.

Respiratory system ≫

The **respiratory system** in the body is concerned with breathing. By breathing, the body can absorb oxygen from the air and release carbon dioxide. This takes place in the **lungs**. Oxygen is needed by the cells in the body for respiration.

We normally breathe air in through the nose. Air passes down the **trachea**, or windpipe, into the lungs. The trachea has rings of cartilage to prevent it from collapsing. You can feel the ridges if you put your thumb at the bottom of your throat just where your ribs start.

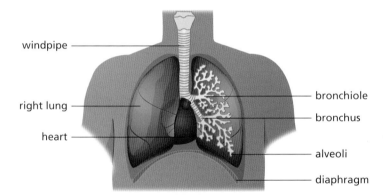

windpipe

right lung

heart

bronchiole

bronchus

alveoli

diaphragm

FIG 5.8 The respiratory system

The trachea divides into two bronchi (singular **bronchus**), one for each lung. Each bronchus further divides into many smaller tubes called **bronchioles**. At the end of each bronchiole is a cluster of tiny air sacs, or alveoli (singular **alveolus**).

The alveoli are well supplied with tiny blood vessels called capillaries. In these sacs, gases are exchanged. Carbon dioxide passes out of the blood into the lung, while oxygen passes from the lung into the blood.

Activity 5.2

Modelling the action of the lungs

Your teacher will assemble the apparatus needed for this activity.

Here is what you need:

- bell jar
- Y tube
- balloons × 2
- elastic band.

Here is what you should do:

1. Connect the balloons to the two forks of a Y-tube using elastic bands.

2. Place the end of the Y-tube through a bung in the bell jar from the inside (see Fig 5.9).

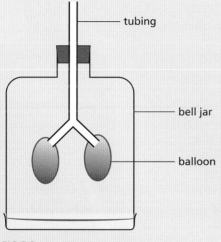

tubing

bell jar

balloon

FIG 5.9

3. Blow through the tube and observe what happens to the balloons.

4. Which part of the apparatus represents:

   a) the lungs?
   b) the trachea?
   c) the bronchi?
   d) the rib cage?

Check your understanding

1. Draw a flow diagram to show the order in which air passes through each of the following to reach the lungs:

   trachea   alveolus   bronchiole   nose   bronchus

Key terms

respiratory system the system of the body that absorbs oxygen and excretes carbon dioxide and water

lung one of a pair of organs in which gases are exchanged

trachea the windpipe that carries air from the nose and mouth into and out of the lungs

bronchus one of two divisions at one end of the trachea that connects with a lung

bronchiole small airways formed by the repeated subdivision of a bronchus

alveolus an air sac found in groups at the end of a bronchiole

Circulatory system

We are learning how to:

- recognise the relationships between specialised cells, tissues, organs and organ systems
- identify parts of the circulatory system.

Circulatory system ⟫⟫

All the cells of the body need a continuous supply of nutrients and oxygen. These nutrients and oxygen dissolve in the blood, which is carried by the **circulatory system**.

The **heart** is the organ at the centre of the circulatory system. It pumps blood around the body. The **arteries** are thick blood vessels that carry blood away from the heart. Arteries are often shown in red on diagrams. The **veins** are thin-walled blood vessels that carry blood towards the heart. Veins are often shown in blue on diagrams.

The circulatory system has two parts – it is a 'double circulation' system. One part sends blood from the heart to the lungs, where the blood receives oxygen and is then returned to the heart. The other part sends blood from the heart to the rest of the body, where the oxygen is used, and the blood is then returned to the heart.

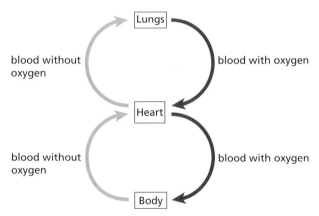

FIG 5.11 Double circulation

Taking a pulse

In order to pump blood around the body, the heart contracts and relaxes many times each minute. Each time the heart contracts, it forces a surge of blood along the arteries.

—— blood in arteries

—— blood in veins

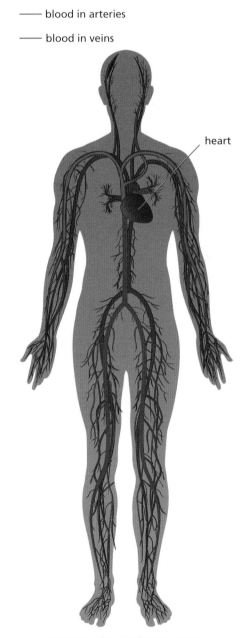

heart

FIG 5.10 The circulatory system

FIG 5.12 Feeling a pulse in **a)** the wrist and **b)** the neck

If you put a fingertip on a point on the body where an artery crosses over a bone, you can feel the regular surge of blood. This is called a pulse. The pulse is most often taken on the wrist or neck.

An average adult has a pulse rate in the range 60–80 beats per minute. This range of values is because people are all a little different.

Activity 5.3

Measuring a person's pulse rate

Before you can measure someone's pulse rate, you need to find that person's pulse. Place your fingers on the inside of the person's wrist. Feel the person's pulse.

Here is what you need:

- stopwatch.

Here is what you should do:

1. Measure your partner's pulse rate by counting the number of pulses in 1 minute. Write the value in a table.
2. Repeat this two more times, so you have taken three measurements in all.
3. Change roles, so now your partner measures your pulse rate.
4. What was your average number of pulses in 1 minute over the three tests?

Check your understanding

1. Which organ is at the centre of the circulatory system?
2. What is the name of the vessels that carry blood away from the heart?
3. What type of blood is pumped from the heart to the lungs?
4. What substances pass from the cells into the blood?

Fun fact

Blood travels around the body very quickly. When you are resting, blood takes about 1 minute to make a complete circuit of the body. When you are exercising, your body needs more nutrients and oxygen, so the blood circulates faster.

Key terms

circulatory system the system that moves blood around the body in order to provide cells with nutrients and oxygen, and to remove waste products

heart the organ that pumps the blood around the circulatory system

artery a large blood vessel that carries blood away from the heart

vein a large blood vessel that carries blood towards the heart

Digestive system

We are learning how to:

- recognise the relationships between specialised cells, tissues, organs and organ systems
- identify parts of the digestive system.

Digestive system ⟫

The **digestive system** in the body obtains nutrients and water from the **foods** we eat.

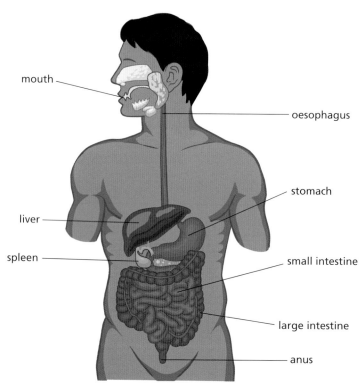

mouth
oesophagus
stomach
liver
spleen
small intestine
large intestine
anus

FIG 5.13 The digestive system

Food consists of complex chemicals that the body cannot absorb directly. During digestion, the food is physically broken down by the action of chewing in the **mouth**, and is chemically broken down by a group of substances called **enzymes**.

Digestion continues in the **stomach** and **small intestine**, where different types of food are broken down. Most of the nutrients produced by digestion are absorbed into the body through the walls of the small intestine. Some water is absorbed in the **large intestine**. What remains passes out of the body as faeces.

Activity 5.4

Tracing the pathway of food through the alimentary canal

Here is what you will need:

- nine rectangular pieces of card, 5 cm × 3 cm.

Here is what you should do:

1. Make name cards for each of the following parts of the digestive system: large intestine, mouth, oesophagus, small intestine, stomach (see Fig 5.14(a)).
2. Make four arrow cards (see Fig 5.14(b)).

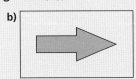

a) Large intestine   b)

FIG 5.14 **a)** Name card; **b)** arrow card

3. Shuffle your cards and then place them on the table, face up.
4. Arrange the name cards and arrow cards to show the order in which food moves through the different parts of the digestive system.

Check your understanding

1. Which part of the digestive system is an organ that is a muscular sac?
2. In which part of the digestive system:
   a) is most water absorbed?
   b) does digestion begin?
   c) does most absorption of nutrients take place?
3. What is the name of the group of substances that break down the complex chemicals in food into simpler substances that can be absorbed?

Key terms

digestive system the system of the body that breaks down food and absorbs the nutrients which are released

food chemical substances that are broken down by the body to obtain nutrients and energy

mouth the first part of the digestive system where food is broken up and moistened, and where digestion starts

enzyme a chemical that helps to break down food

stomach an organ in the digestive system where food is held while digestion takes place

small intestine part of the digestive system where most absorption of nutrients takes place

large intestine part of the digestive system where water is absorbed

Excretory system

We are learning how to:

- recognise the relationships between specialised cells, tissues, organs and organ systems
- identify parts of the excretory system.

Excretory system 》》》

Excretion is the removal from the body of waste products produced by **metabolic processes**. The metabolic processes are those that occur inside the body and that are essential for life.

Note that excretion does not include the loss of faeces from the body. Faeces are not formed by metabolic processes but are what is left after food has been digested. The correct term for the loss of faeces from the body is 'egestion'.

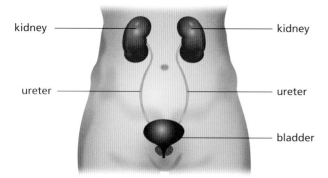

kidney — kidney

ureter — ureter

bladder

FIG 5.15 The excretory system

The main organs of the **excretory system** are the **kidneys**. The kidneys filter out soluble waste products from the blood and send them to the **bladder** where they are stored and then expelled from the body as **urine**.

Excretion is not limited to the kidneys. The lungs also play a role in excretion. You have already seen how **carbon dioxide** gas passes from the blood into the lungs during breathing. Carbon dioxide is an excretory product formed during respiration.

The **skin** is also an important organ of excretion. Some of the water formed during respiration is lost through the skin during **sweating**. This water contains excess salt and urea (a waste product of the metabolism of proteins). Urea gives the body an unpleasant smell when we sweat.

> **Fun fact**
>
> People who have diseased or damaged kidneys can undergo a kidney transplant operation in which their kidneys are replaced by healthy kidneys, obtained from a person who has recently died. The first kidney transplant took place in 1950.

Activity 5.5

Excreting carbon dioxide

Here is what you need:

- boiling tubes with bungs × 2
- tubing
- T-piece
- limewater
- stand and clamp × 2.

Here is what you should do:

1. Arrange the apparatus as shown in Fig 5.16. It is important that the tubes going into the boiling tubes are the correct length and in the places shown.
2. Pour limewater into each boiling tube until it is about half full.
3. Slowly breathe in and out through the mouthpiece.

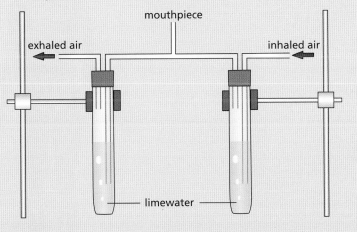

FIG 5.16

4. Limewater turns cloudy in the presence of carbon dioxide gas. In which boiling tube does the limewater turn cloudy first?
5. What can you deduce about the concentration of carbon dioxide in exhaled air compared with that in inhaled air?

Check your understanding

1. What is excretion?
2. Give one example of a substance that the body excretes.
3. Why is the loss of faeces from the body not an example of excretion?
4. Name three organs involved in excretion.

Key terms

metabolic process a process in the body that is essential for life

excretory system the system that removes the waste products of metabolism from the body

kidney one of a pair of organs that removes waste substances and some water from the blood

bladder a muscular sac that stores urine ready for excretion

urine a solution of waste substances, like urea and unwanted salts in water, that is expelled from the body at regular intervals

carbon dioxide a gas found in the air, which is made during respiration and combustion, and used up during photosynthesis

skin the outermost covering of the body that is sensitive to certain stimuli and also has a function in excretion

sweat a solution of urea and salts in water that is excreted through pores in the skin, especially during exercise or when the weather is warm

Skeletal and muscular systems

We are learning how to:

- recognise the relationships between specialised cells, tissues, organs and organ systems
- identify parts of the skeletal and muscular system.

Skeletal and muscular systems

The body is built around a framework of bones. These bones form the **skeletal system**, or **skeleton**. The skeleton contains 206 bones. The various muscles of the **muscular system** are attached to these bones.

The skeleton gives our body its shape and protects some of the organs. The skull protects the brain, while the ribcage protects the heart and lungs.

The skeleton also provides a framework of bones to which muscles attach. Muscles make it possible for the bones of the skeleton to move. Movement takes place at **joints** where bones meet.

For example, the action of muscles in the upper arm allows the arm to bend at the elbow joint. When one muscle relaxes and the other contracts, the arm bends at the elbow. When the roles of the muscles are reversed, the arm straightens.

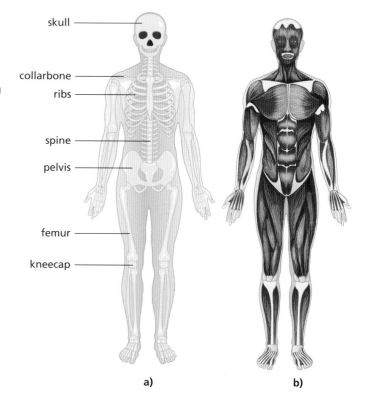

skull
collarbone
ribs
spine
pelvis
femur
kneecap

a) b)

FIG 5.17 **a)** Skeletal system; **b)** muscular system

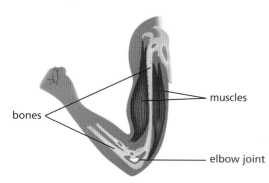

muscles
bones
elbow joint

FIG 5.18 Muscles make it possible for bones to move at joints

Activity 5.6

Modelling a hinge joint

A hinge joint is the type of joint you have at your elbow, at your knee and between the bones of your fingers.

Here is what you will need:

- lengths of dowel or pencils 15 cm long × 2
- sticky tape.
- thin card

Here is what you should do:

1. Wind a piece of thin card about 5 cm square around a dowel to make it into a tube.
2. Slide the tube down the dowel so that about 2 cm of the dowel is covered.
3. Use sticky tape to fix the tube onto the dowel.
4. Slide a second dowel into the other end of the tube until about 2 cm of dowel is covered.
5. Use sticky tape to fix the tube onto the second dowel.

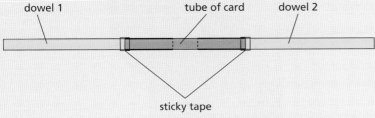

FIG 5.19

6. Flatten the part of the cardboard tube between the dowels.
7. Bend the flattened part of the tube so the dowels come together.
8. How does the movement of the dowels resemble the movement of the bones in your arm?
9. In what way is the flattened tube like the hinge on a door?

Check your understanding

1. Fig 5.20 is an X-ray of the bones at a joint.

   a) In which part of the body do you think this joint is found?

   b) What makes it possible for the bones to move at a joint?

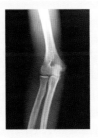

FIG 5.20

Fun fact

The longest bone is the femur, which is at the top of the leg, between the thigh and the knee. The smallest bone is inside the ear.

Key terms

skeletal system the system of the body consisting of a framework of bones that gives the body its shape

skeleton another name for the skeletal system

muscular system a collection of muscles connected to the skeleton, which makes movement possible

joint a place where two bones meet and can move relative to each other

Reproductive system

We are learning how to:

- recognise the relationships between specialised cells, tissues, organs and organ systems
- identify parts of the reproductive system.

Reproductive system

The **reproductive system** is concerned with producing young. Unlike the other systems you have learned about, the parts of the reproductive system are different in males and females.

Male reproductive system

Key term

reproductive system the part of the body involved in reproduction

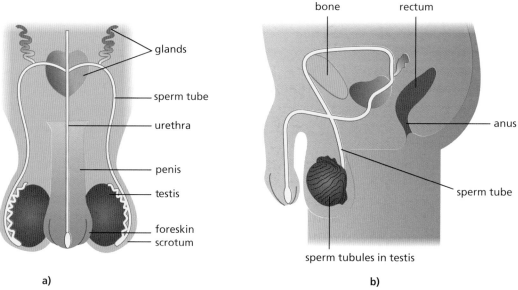

FIG 5.21 Male reproductive system from **a)** the front and **b)** the side

The sex organs in the male reproductive system are the testes (singular **testis**), which produce the sperm. The testes are held in a sack called the scrotum. The testes hang outside the body. Being outside the body keeps the testes below body temperature, which is necessary for sperm production.

Sperm are produced all the time and stored in tiny tubes outside the testes. The sperm eventually pass into the sperm tube and out of the body along the **urethra** and through the **penis**.

The glands have an important role in releasing a fluid that keeps the sperm alive when they pass out of the body. The mixture of sperm and fluid is semen.

Fun fact

The human reproductive system functions only after we reach a certain age. For girls, this is usually between 10 and 15 years, and for boys between 11 and 16 years. The time when a person becomes sexually mature is called puberty.

Female reproductive system

The female reproductive system is different from the male reproductive system, because it performs a different role.

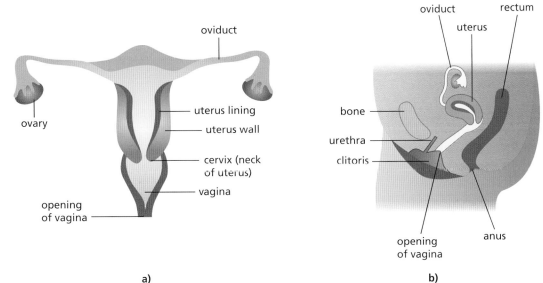

a)

b)

FIG 5.22 Female reproductive system from a) the front and b) the side

The **ovaries** are the female sex organs, and produce eggs. The ovaries are attached to the inside of the abdomen, just a little below the kidneys.

Once a girl becomes sexually mature, the ovaries release an egg approximately every 28 days. This is called ovulation. The egg passes into the funnel-shaped opening of the oviduct, and from there travels along the oviduct to the **uterus**, or womb.

If the egg is not fertilised, it will eventually pass out of the body through the cervix and **vagina** together with some of the thickened uterus wall. If the egg is fertilised, it will implant itself in the thickened wall of the uterus and develop into a baby over the following 9 months.

Check your understanding

1. Which parts of the male reproductive system are:

   a) outside the body?

   b) inside the body?

2. Which parts of the female reproductive system are:

   a) outside the body?

   b) inside the body?

Key terms

testis one of a pair of organs that produce sperm

urethra a duct through which urine is expelled from the bladder and out of the body

penis the part of the male reproductive system through which sperm passes out

ovary one of a pair of organs in which ova (eggs) are produced

uterus the part of the female reproductive system, sometimes called the womb, in which a fertilised ovum becomes embedded and develops into an embryo

vagina the part of the female reproductive system that is open to the outside

Specialised animal cells

We are learning how to:

- recognise the relationships between specialised cells, tissues, organs and organ systems
- identify specialised animal cells.

Specialised animal cells ▶▶

The various types of cells in the human body have different shapes and appearances. This is because they have different jobs to do.

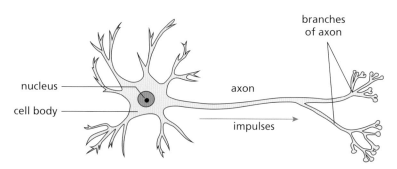

FIG 5.23 Nerve cell, or neuron

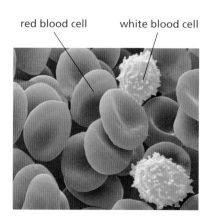

FIG 5.24 Red and white blood cells

Nerve cells, or **neurons**, carry electrical impulses from one place to another in the body.

Red blood cells carry oxygen around the body. They are red because they contain a pigment called haemoglobin, and have a characteristic 'doughnut' shape.

White blood cells attack and kill invading germs that would make us ill. One type of white blood cell kills germs by releasing chemicals, while another wraps itself around the germs and digests them.

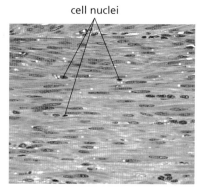

FIG 5.25 Smooth muscle cells

Smooth muscle is found in many places in the body. It is different from the striated muscle found in the arms and legs. **Smooth muscle cells** are long and thin. The muscle is able to contract by making the cells shorter.

The **sperm** is the male reproductive cell. After intercourse, the sperm must swim up the female reproductive system until it finds an ovum. It does this by wriggling its tail, or flagellum.

FIG 5.26 Male reproductive cell, or sperm

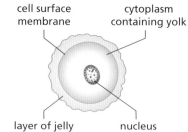

FIG 5.27 Female reproductive cell, or ovum

The **ovum** (plural ova) is the female reproductive cell. Ova cannot move like sperm, but are much larger. Each ovum contains yolk, which will nourish the zygote formed when a sperm penetrates the cell.

Activity 5.7

Animal cells, tissues, organs and systems

You will not need any equipment or materials for this activity.

Here is what you should do:

1. Copy and complete Table 5.1 with the names of the missing cells, tissues, organs and systems.

Cells	Tissue	Organ	System
			respiratory
	heart muscle		
		kidney	
sperm, ovum			

TABLE 5.1

Check your understanding

1. Fig 5.28 shows some of the cells in the lining of the throat.

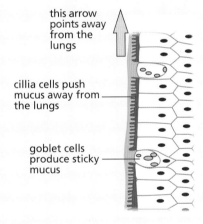

this arrow points away from the lungs

cillia cells push mucus away from the lungs

goblet cells produce sticky mucus

FIG 5.28

a) Name two types of specialised cell shown in Fig 5.28.

b) Suggest how these types of cell prevent particles that we breathe in from entering the lungs.

Key terms

nerve cell a cell that carries nerve impulses

neuron another name for a nerve cell

red blood cell a blood cell that carries oxygen around the body

white blood cell a blood cell that fights germs that invade the body

smooth muscle cells the type of cells from which heart tissue is formed

sperm the human male sex cell (plural 'sperm')

ovum the human female sex cell (plural 'ova')

Plant systems

We are learning how to:

- recognise the relationships between specialised cells, tissues, organs and organ systems
- identify systems in a flowering plant.

Plant systems >>>

Plants also have systems. The part that you can see above the ground is the shoot system, and the part you cannot see, because it is buried in the soil, is the root system. Each system has a different role.

All flowering plants have five important organs: **roots**, a **stem**, **leaves**, **flowers** and **fruits**. Each of these is important to the survival of the plant.

Roots

The roots of a plant are buried in the soil. Roots:

- hold the plant in the soil, so it is not blown about in the wind

- absorb water containing minerals from the soil

- can store starch for the plant.

Plant roots often have lateral root branches.

Roots have root hairs on their surface to absorb water.

Stem

The stem of a plant connects the roots to the leaves and flowers, above the ground. The stem:

- supports the parts of the plant above the ground

- allows substances to move around the plant.

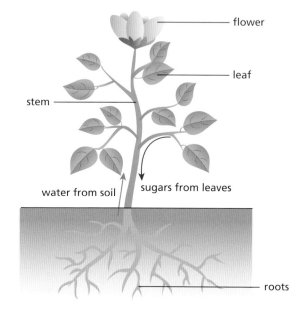

FIG 5.29 Parts of a flowering plant

Activity 5.8

Examining the tubes that carry water up a stem

Here is what you need:

- solution of red ink (several drops of ink added to water in a container)
- stalk of celery or Shiny Bush.

Here is what you should do:

1. At the start of a lesson, take a freshly gathered celery stalk. Cut off the bottom and stand the stalk in the red ink solution.
2. Near the end of the lesson, take the stalk out of the ink solution. Cut across the middle with a sharp knife.
3. Examine the cut part of the celery. Can you see any red dots where the stalk has drawn up the ink?

FIG 5.31 Ferns in the Sangre Grande forest

Ferns reproduce in a different way to flowering plants. They produce spores instead of seeds.

Leaves

The leaves are usually the most obvious part of a plant.

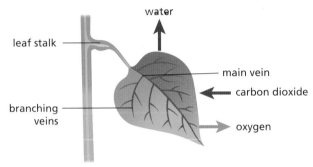

FIG 5.30 Parts of a leaf

Leaves are green because they contain chlorophyll, which is a green pigment.

The leaves:

- make nutrients by the process of photosynthesis
- allow the plant to absorb carbon dioxide for photosynthesis and release oxygen formed in this process
- lose water vapour in a process called transpiration.

Flowers

Flowers are the organs of sexual reproduction of a flowering plant. When a plant reproduces, it forms fruits and seeds.

Fruits

Fruits contain the seeds of the plant. They are sometimes eaten by animals, which helps the plant to disperse its seeds.

Check your understanding

1. Why is it better for a plant to have a network of many roots spread out in the surrounding soil than just a single root?
2. Why are the stem and leaves of a plant green, but the roots are not?

Key terms

root the part of a plant below the ground that anchors the plant, and absorbs water and nutrients from the soil

stem the part of a plant above ground that has leaves, and sometimes produces flowers

leaf the flat green part of a plant that traps sunlight and carries out photosynthesis

flower the organ of sexual reproduction in plants

fruit the part of a plant that forms around the maturing seeds of the plant

Specialised plant cells

We are learning how to:

- recognise the relationships between specialised cells, tissues, organs and organ systems
- identify specialised plant cells.

Specialised plant cells 》》》

Plants have specialised cells in the same way as animals do. Each type of cell carries out a particular function within the plant.

Palisade cells

Palisade cells are found in leaves, beneath the outer epidermis, and often make up most of the leaf.

Palisade cells are vertically elongated and contain chloroplasts. The palisade cells absorb most of the light energy that the leaf uses in photosynthesis.

Guard cells

Guard cells are in the underside of leaves. A pair of **guard cells** surrounds each opening, or **stoma** (plural **stomata**).

The guard cells help to regulate the rate at which a plant loses water through its leaves, by opening and closing the stomata.

When the guard cells absorb water they swell and the stoma opens, allowing the plant to lose water. When the guard cells lose water they shrink. This closes the stoma, preventing the plant from losing any more water.

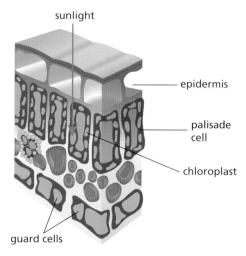

FIG 5.32 A section through the leaf of a plant, to show the specialised types of cell

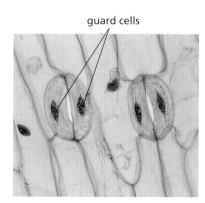

FIG 5.33 Guard cells in the underside of a leaf

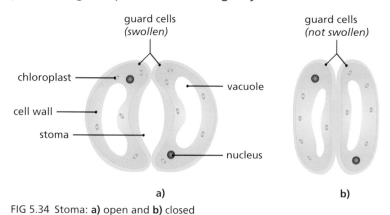

FIG 5.34 Stoma: **a)** open and **b)** closed

Activity 5.9

Plant organs and their functions

You will not need any equipment or materials for this activity.

Here is what you should do:

1. Copy and complete Table 5.2 with the missing organs and functions.

Organ	Function
leaves	
	sexual reproduction
stem	
	absorbs water and nutrients
	contains seeds

TABLE 5.2

Root hair cells

Root hair cells are present in the roots of plants. The root hairs are not hairs like you have on your head, but a hair-shaped part of a root cell that grows out into the soil.

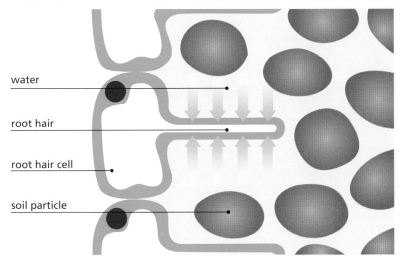

water

root hair

root hair cell

soil particle

FIG 5.35 Root hair cell

The root hair greatly increases the surface area of the root, making it easier for the plant to absorb water from the soil.

Check your understanding

1. With the help of suitable diagrams, explain how guard cells control the loss of water from a leaf.

Fun fact

Plant cells have a rigid cell wall made of cellulose that surrounds them. People cannot digest cellulose, so when we eat plant material, the cellulose remains. This undigested cellulose is the main constituent of fibre, or roughage, in our diet.

Key terms

palisade cell a cell in the leaf of a plant that contains chloroplasts

guard cell one of a pair of cells that surround a stoma, and open and close it

stoma an opening in a leaf that allows gases to pass in and out

stomata plural of stoma

root hair cell a hair-shaped cell at the end of a root that has a large surface area to assist absorption

Unit 6: Cellular processes – diffusion

We are learning how to:

- describe how substances move into and out of cells.

Diffusion »

You already know something about the process of **diffusion**, although you may never have heard it called by this name. Living things need to move substances around. One way in which this is done is by diffusion. Sometimes when you step into your home, you know that someone has been baking or cooking.

When someone is baking or cooking, tiny particles of food move through the air. The particles travel in the air from the kitchen to all the other rooms in your home. We call this spreading out of particles 'diffusion'.

FIG 6.1 Spicy meat, Trinidad style

Activity 6.1

Investigating diffusion

Your teacher will help you with this activity.

Here is what you need:

- shallow open container like a watch glass
- volatile liquid that has a characteristic smell, like a perfume
- stopwatch with a second hand.

Here is what you should do:

1. Students sit or stand in rows at different distances from the teacher's table.

2. The teacher will pour a small amount of perfume onto a watch glass on the table at the front of the class.

teacher's table — perfume in watch glass

rows of students

FIG 6.2

3. Each student should raise his or her arm and note the time when he or she first smells the perfume.

4. Which students were first to smell the perfume?

5. Which students were last to smell the perfume?

In Activity 6.1, the perfume spreads out, or diffuses, from the watch glass to all parts of the classroom. At the start, the perfume is at a high **concentration** immediately above the watch glass and at a low concentration in the rest of the classroom. The perfume particles move from the region of high concentration to regions of low concentration.

We say that the perfume particles diffuse across a **concentration gradient**. A concentration gradient is the difference in the concentration of particles between two regions.

After a while, the concentration of perfume particles is the same in all parts of the room.

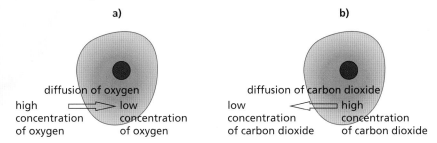

FIG 6.3 Diffusion of gases **a)** into and **b)** out of cells

Substances diffuse into and out of cells across concentration gradients. For example:

- The concentration of oxygen in the blood is higher than in the cell, where it is used up during respiration, so oxygen diffuses from the blood into the cell.

- The concentration of carbon dioxide in the cell is higher, because it is produced during respiration, so carbon dioxide diffuses from the cell into the blood.

(Respiration is covered in Unit 3.)

> **Fun fact**
>
> Diffusion takes place through solids, but this happens much more slowly than through liquids and gases.

Key terms

diffusion the spreading out of particles of a substance to fill the space available

concentration the number of particles of a substance per unit volume (for example, in a solution, g/cm^3 of water)

concentration gradient the difference in the concentration of particles of a substance in one place compared to another place

Check your understanding

1. Fig 6.4 shows what happened when a crystal of potassium manganate(VII) was placed in a beaker of water and left for 24 hours.

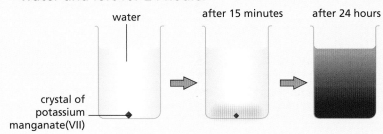

water   after 15 minutes   after 24 hours

crystal of potassium manganate(VII)

FIG 6.4

Explain why the appearance of the water changed.

Osmosis

We are learning how to:

• describe how substances move into and out of cells.

Osmosis ⟫⟫

Osmosis is a special kind of diffusion that is concerned only with the movement of water molecules. Like other substances, water diffuses along a concentration gradient from a place where water is in high concentration to a place where it is in low concentration.

This can sometimes be a little confusing, because water is in a higher concentration in a dilute solution and in a lower concentration in a concentrated solution. What we are saying, therefore, is that under suitable conditions water will move from a dilute solution, making it more concentrated, to a concentrated solution, making it more dilute.

A **differentially permeable membrane** is a membrane with holes that are large enough to allow small molecules like water to pass through, but small enough to prevent the movement of large molecules.

Fig 6.5 shows what happens if we separate pure water from a solution of a compound by using a differentially permeable membrane. Notice that the water molecules move in both directions through the differentially permeable membrane. However, more water molecules pass from the dilute solution to the concentrated solution than pass in the other direction. Eventually the concentration of the solution reaches an **equilibrium** situation and remains unchanged.

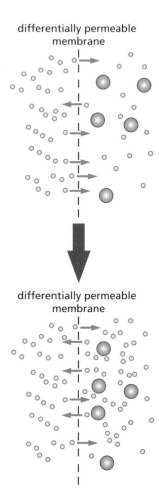

differentially permeable membrane

differentially permeable membrane

FIG 6.5 Movement of particles across a differentially permeable membrane

Activity 6.2

Investigating osmosis

Here is what you need:

• fresh fruit – mango or paw-paw

• knife

• shallow dish

• sugar.

Here is what you should do:

1. Peel the fruit with a knife and cut it in half. If you are using a mango or a paw-paw, remove the seeds to make a well.

2. Cut the outside of each half of the fruit to make a flat surface for it to stand on.

FIG 6.6

3. Stand each half of the fruit on its flat part in a shallow bowl of distilled water so that the well is at the top. In one of the fruit halves, just cover the bottom of the well with a layer of sugar but do not fill the well.

4. Do not put any sugar in the well of the other half of the fruit.

5. Leave the halves of fruit in the water for 30 minutes.

6. After 30 minutes, record your observations.

7. Explain your observations in terms of osmosis.

In Activity 6.2 the sugar dissolves in one half of the fruit, forming a sugar solution. The concentration of water in the dish is greater than the concentration of water in the sugar solution, so water passes from the dish into the fruit, through the fruit cells, by osmosis.

Water passes into and out of all living cells by osmosis. The process of osmosis controls the concentration of substances in the cell.

Key terms

osmosis diffusion that involves water molecules

differentially permeable membrane a membrane that allows some particles to pass through it but not others

equilibrium a situation in which the movement of particles in one direction is equal to the movement of particles in the opposite direction

Check your understanding

1. Visking tubing is a differentially permeable membrane. Fig 6.7 shows a bag made of Visking tubing, filled with 20% sugar solution and suspended in a beaker of distilled water.

   a) Predict what will happen to the level of liquid in the glass tube if the apparatus is left to stand for 30 minutes.

   b) Explain your answer to **a)**.

   c) Predict what will happen if the same apparatus is used but distilled water is placed in the Visking bag and sugar solution in the beaker.

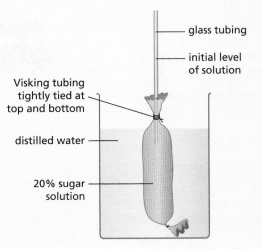

FIG 6.7

Photosynthesis

We are learning how to:

- describe the process of photosynthesis.

Photosynthesis ⟫⟫

Photosynthesis is the process by which green plants make food. To carry out photosynthesis, plants must obtain **energy** from sunlight.

Plant leaves are green because the cells contain a special pigment called **chlorophyll**. This pigment is able to trap some of the sunlight that falls on the leaf, and use it for photosynthesis.

FIG 6.8 Green plants obtain energy from sunlight

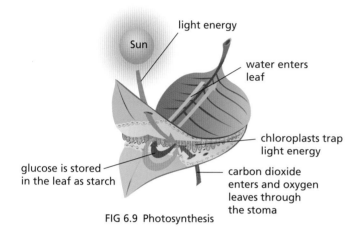

FIG 6.9 Photosynthesis

light energy

Sun

water enters leaf

chloroplasts trap light energy

glucose is stored in the leaf as starch

carbon dioxide enters and oxygen leaves through the stoma

Carbon dioxide diffuses into leaves from the atmosphere and **water** enters leaves from the ground through the plant roots and stem. **Oxygen** is released into the atmosphere, and the **glucose** is stored in the leaf as starch until it is needed elsewhere in the plant.

$$\text{carbon dioxide} + \text{water} \xrightarrow[\text{chlorophyll}]{\text{sunlight}} \text{glucose} + \text{oxygen}$$

Activity 6.3

Testing a leaf for starch

Here is what you need:

- green leaf
- test tube
- beaker of hot water
- iodine solution
- tweezers
- white tile
- ethanol
- pipette.

Here is what you should do:

1. Using tweezers, hold the leaf in hot water for about 1 minute.

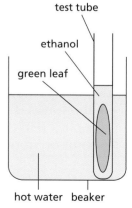

test tube

ethanol

green leaf

hot water   beaker

FIG 6.10

2. Fold the leaf and place it in a test tube. Pour sufficient ethanol into the test tube to cover the leaf.

3. Stand the test tube in hot water for about 10 minutes. Give the test tube an occasional shake.

4. Take the leaf out of the test tube and wash it in cold water.

5. Spread the leaf on a tile and add a few drops of iodine solution using a teat pipette.

6. What colour does the iodine solution turn? What does this show you?

Green plants, either directly or indirectly, provide food for all other organisms on Earth.

- Herbivores feed directly on green plants.

- Carnivores feed on herbivores.

- Omnivores feed on plants and animals that eat plants.

- Decomposers break down waste or dead animal and vegetable material.

Check your understanding

1. Joseph carried out an investigation into the effects of temperature and light intensity on the rate of photosynthesis in tomato plants. The results are shown in Fig 6.11.

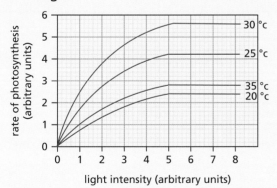

FIG 6.11

a) At which temperature and light intensity is the rate of photosynthesis greatest?

b) Why do the curves flatten out at about 5 units of light at all temperatures?

Fun fact

Photosynthesis is not a very efficient process. Typically, only between 1 and 2% of sunlight is used by plants in photosynthesis.

Key terms

photosynthesis the process in plants by which carbon dioxide and water are converted to glucose using energy from sunlight

energy the ability to do work

chlorophyll a green pigment found in the green parts of plants that traps energy from sunlight for use in photosynthesis

carbon dioxide a gas found in the air, which is made during respiration and combustion, and used up during photosynthesis

water a liquid required by all forms of life to survive

oxygen a gas found in the air, which is made during photosynthesis, and used up during respiration and combustion

glucose a simple sugar

Review of Living things

Characteristics of living things

- All organisms exhibit seven characteristics that we associate with living things. These characteristics are:
  - Growth
  - Respiration
  - Irritability
  - Movement
  - Nutrition
  - Excretion
  - Reproduction.

  If we take the first letter of each of these characteristics, it spells GRIMNER.

- All organisms are composed of cells.
  - Unicellular organisms consist of only a single cell.
  - Multicellular organisms consist of many cells.

Cells

- Cells are so small they we can only see them with the aid of a microscope. In order to make the parts of a cell easier to see, we stain specimens of cells with dyes.

- A simple animal cell consists of:
  - a nucleus, which controls the processes that go on in the cell and contains chromosomes
  - cytoplasm, in which there are mitochondria that provide the cell with energy, glycogen grains and small vacuoles
  - a cell membrane, which controls the movement of substances into and out of the cell.

- A simple plant cell is similar in structure to an animal cell, but it contains some additional features:
  - a rigid cell wall made of cellulose that gives the cell shape
  - chloroplasts containing the green pigment chlorophyll, which traps the energy needed for photosynthesis from sunlight
  - starch grains in place of glycogen grains
  - large vacuoles in place of small vacuoles.

- Both animal and plant cells have a cell membrane. A plant cell has an additional cell wall.

- Cells are the building blocks from which all organisms are formed. Complex organisms contain many different types of cell. These cells are arranged in tissues, the tissues form parts of an organ, and the organ forms part of an organ system.

cells ⟶ tissues ⟶ organs ⟶ systems ⟶ organism

- The human body contains a number of important systems. Table 6.1 shows the main organs in some of these systems.

System	Main organ(s)
circulatory system	heart
respiratory system	lungs
digestive system	stomach, intestines, liver
excretory system	kidneys, skin, lungs
skeletal and muscular system	skeleton, muscles
reproductive system	testes, ovaries

TABLE 6.1 Systems and main organs of the human body

- Complex organisms have specialised cells that have particular functions within the organism.

- Specialised cells in humans include: neurons, or nerve cells; red and white blood cells; sex cells (sperm and ovum); and smooth muscle cells.

- Specialised cells in a flowering plant include: palisade cells, guard cells, root hair cells and sex cells (pollen and ovum).

Diffusion and osmosis

- Diffusion is the movement of particles from a region of higher concentration to a region of lower concentration along a concentration gradient. Substances pass into and out of cells by diffusion.

- Osmosis is a special kind of diffusion, which involves the movement of water particles. During osmosis, water molecules move from a more dilute solution to a more concentrated solution through a differentially permeable membrane. Water passes into and out of cells by osmosis.

Photosynthesis

- Photosynthesis is the process by which green plants trap energy from sunlight and use it to convert carbon dioxide and water into glucose. Oxygen is an important by-product of this process.

carbon dioxide + water + energy ⟶ glucose + oxygen

Review questions on Living things

1. Fig 6.12 shows some birds in a nest.

   List the seven characteristics of birds that indicate to you that they are living organisms and not non-living objects. Write a sentence about each characteristic.

   FIG 6.12

2. Fig 6.13 shows a typical plant cell.

   a) Name parts A–F on the diagram.

   b) Say whether each of the following statements about cells is true or false:

   i) Animal cells have a cell wall made of cellulose.

   ii) The nucleus controls many of the processes in the cell.

   iii) Mitochondria are found in the cytoplasm.

   iv) Plant cells store food as grains of glycogen.

   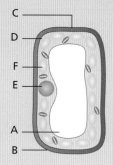

   FIG 6.13

3. Table 6.2 lists some cell parts. Copy and complete the table, as follows. Decide whether each part is found: only in animal cells (write A next to it in the table), only in plant cells (write P) or in both types of cell (write B).

Part of a cell	Write A, P or B
cell membrane	
cell wall	
chloroplast	
cytoplasm	
nucleus	
large vacuole	
mitochondria	
glycogen grains	

TABLE 6.2

4. Fig 6.14 shows a unicellular organism called *Euglena*.

Euglena lives in water and is able to move using a whip-like flagellum.

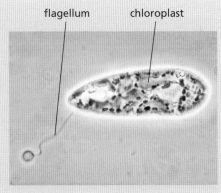

flagellum   chloroplast

FIG 6.14

  a) What does 'unicellular' mean?

  b) Suggest one way in which *Euglena* is like:

    i)   a plant

    ii) an animal.

  c) Suggest why organisms like *Euglena* are no longer classified as plants or animals, but are placed in a separate group.

5. A person's breathing rate is the number of times they breathe in and out each minute. Table 6.3 shows the range of breathing rates for people of different ages.

  a) What general trend do the data show?

  b) Present the data as a bar chart. Use the height of the bars to show the breathing rate.

Age in years	Typical breathing rate in breaths per minute
up to 1	30–40
1 to 3	25–35
3 to 6	20–30
6 to 12	18–26
over 12	12–20

TABLE 6.3

6. Fig 6.15 shows the pulse rates of a fit person and an unfit person before, during and after exercise.

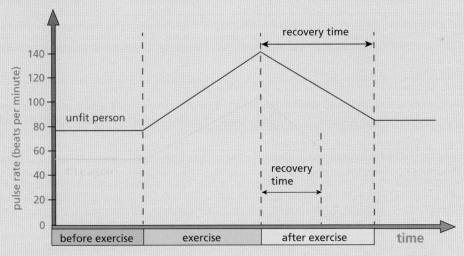

FIG 6.15

  a) What was the pulse rate of the unfit person:

    i)   before exercise?

    ii) at the end of the exercise period?

  b) How does the pulse rate of a fit person compare with the pulse rate of an unfit person:

    i)   at rest?

    ii) when exercising?

c) i) What difference is there between the recovery time of a fit person compared with that of an unfit person?

   ii) Suggest a reason for the difference in **i)** above.

7. a) Name the parts A–E of the female reproductive system shown in Fig 6.16.

   b) In which of parts A–E:

   i) are eggs released?

   ii) do fertilised eggs usually develop during pregnancy?

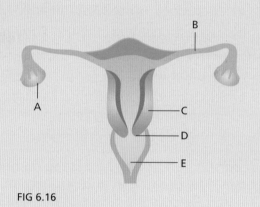

FIG 6.16

8. Fig 6.17 shows two specialised cells from the human body.

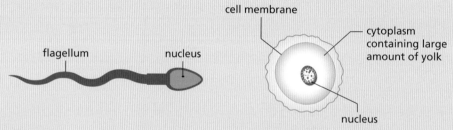

FIG 6.17

   a) Identify cells A and B.

   b) Describe one way in which the structure of each cell is suited to its role in the body.

9. A student carried out an investigation in which she placed 1 cm and 2 cm cubes of clear agar gel in potassium manganate(VII) solution for 30 minutes. After this time she removed the cubes and cut them in half. Fig 6.18 shows what she observed. The purple colour shows how far the potassium manganate(VII) solution had reached.

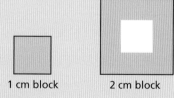

1 cm block   2 cm block

FIG 6.18

   a) By what process has the potassium manganate(VII) moved into the blocks of agar gel?

   b) Explain why the potassium manganate(VII) has reached the centre of the 1 cm block but not the centre of the 2 cm block.

10. a) Copy and complete the word equation for photosynthesis.

$$\text{.......... + water} \xrightarrow[\text{chlorophyll}]{\text{........................}} \text{glucose + ...}$$

b) Describe the test for the presence of starch in a leaf.

c) The plant shown in Fig 6.19 is unusual because part of the stem and the leaves attached to it are white. The remainder of the plant is green.

Predict whether you would expect a leaf from the white part of the stem and a leaf from the green part of the stem to give a positive test for starch. Explain your answer.

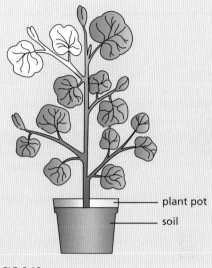

plant pot

soil

FIG 6.19

Estimating the sugar content of sweet potato

Sweet potatoes are a popular food in the Caribbean. They are eaten in lots of different ways, including boiled, mashed, baked and as fries.

100 g of sweet potato contains about 20 g of carbohydrates, 1.6 g of protein and 0.1 g fat. It is also a good source of vitamins A, B_6, B_{12}, C and D, and of the minerals calcium, iron and magnesium.

As the name 'sweet potato' suggests, a proportion of the 20 g of carbohydrates is present as sugar. This information will be useful to someone wanting to reduce their sugar intake.

FIG 6.20 Sweet potatoes

1. You are going to work in groups of three or four to estimate the concentration of sugar in sweet potatoes using osmosis. Your tasks are:

   • to revise the work carried out on osmosis in this unit so that you understand the process

   • to prepare sugar solutions of different concentrations

   • to measure the mass gain or mass loss when sweet potato chips are soaked in sugar solutions of different concentrations

   • to draw a graph of mass gain/loss against concentration and use it to deduce the sugar concentration in sweet potatoes.

a) Osmosis is a special kind of diffusion involving water molecules. When solutions of different concentrations are separated by a differentially permeable membrane there is a net movement of water molecules from the less concentrated solution to the more concentrated solution. Eventually the solutions will have the same concentration.

   Read through the work you carried out in Topic 6.2 Osmosis to make sure that you understand this process.

b) Make up sugar solutions of different concentrations. The percentage of sugar in sweet potato is between 0 and 10% so you should make up solutions of 0%, 1%, ..., 10% by mass of sugar.

   To make up each solution:

   • Place a clean, dry 250 cm³ beaker on a balance.

   • Press the tare/zero key to zero the display.

   • Add sugar to the required mass.

   • Top up with distilled water until the display reads 100 g.

FIG 6.21 Making up solutions

Place some cling wrap over the solution to prevent water evaporating or being absorbed from the air before you use the solution. Make sure you label each beaker with the concentration of sugar solution it contains.

c) From one or more peeled sweet potato cut 55 chips of similar thickness

The chips should not be too thick. This shape provides a large surface area for osmosis to take place.

FIG 6.22 Sweet potato chips

d) Use a spreadsheet to record the following data.

Weigh a batch of five chips and record the mass. Place the chips in 0% sugar solution Repeat this for each concentration up to 10% sugar solution.

Leave the chips overnight. The following day remove each batch of five chips from each solution, wipe them to remove surface solution and then reweigh them. Record the mass.

Use the spreadsheet to calculate the change in mass and the percentage change in mass for each batch.

e) Use the data you have collected to plot a graph of percentage mass gained or lost on the y-axis against concentration of sugar in the solution on the x-axis.

Draw the straight line of best fit through the points and find the concentration at which there would be no increase or decrease in the mass of sweet potato chips. This is your estimate of the concentration of sugar in sweet potatoes.

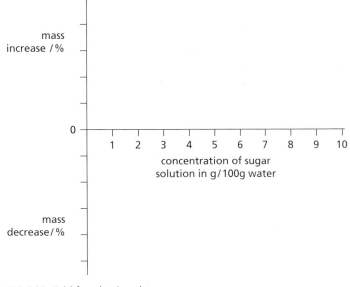

FIG 6.23 Grid for plotting data

f) Prepare a PowerPoint presentation in which you should focus on the results you obtained and make suggestions as to how people might use your results. You might pose questions like:

- What is the daily recommended intake of sugar?
- How many spoonsful of sugar does a typical sweet potato contain?
- Should sweet potato be something you eat every day?

As part of your presentation you might hold up a sweet potato and an equivalent mass of sugar to emphasise how much sugar the potato contains.

Unit 7: Properties of matter

We are learning how to:

- investigate some properties of matter
- show that matter occupies space
- show that matter has mass.

What is matter? »

Matter is everything around you that has mass and occupies **space**. Matter can be in one of three forms: a **solid**, a **liquid** or a **gas**. For example, water and gasoline are liquids at room temperature, and rocks, iron and glass are solids. They all occupy space and have mass. Air is a gas, but even air has mass and occupies space, even though its mass is very small.

a) the sea

b) gasoline being pumped into a car

c) rocks

d) iron bars

e) glass used in a building

FIG 7.1 Matter is all around us, in many different forms

Differences between solids, liquids and gases

Solids are generally rigid, hard and heavy. A concrete block is a solid: it is **rigid**, which means you cannot change its

Key terms

matter everything possessing mass and volume

space the volume occupied by matter

solid the form of a substance with a rigid structure and set volume

liquid the form of a substance with no rigid structure but a set volume

shape easily, it is hard and it is heavy. However, not all solids are rigid, hard and heavy (see Fig 7.2).

Liquids are not rigid. They can **flow** or be poured. Some solids can be poured, but they are not liquids (see Fig 7.3(a)). Liquids are not usually shiny like solid metals, but one metal is a liquid at room temperature (see Fig 7.3(b)).

a)

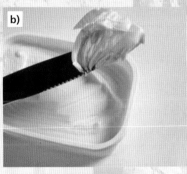
b)

a)

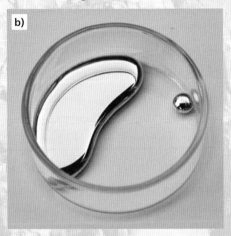
b)

FIG 7.3 **a)** Granulated sugar can be poured, but it is not a liquid.
b) Mercury is a metal and is shiny, but it is a liquid

Gases are very light and they are not rigid. Many gases are invisible.

FIG 7.2 **a)** Polystyrene is not heavy, but it is solid. **b)** Margarine is not rigid, but it is solid

a)

b)

FIG 7.4 **a)** Air is invisible, so how do we know it is there? **b)** We can see these gases used on stage during a rock show, and we can see that they flow

Check your understanding

1. List two properties for each of:

   a) solids
   b) liquids
   c) gases.

2. We know water can exist in all three states of matter. Name the three states of matter of water.

Key terms

gas the form of a substance with neither a rigid structure nor a set volume

rigid firm and set in place

flow the continuous movement of a fluid material

Properties of gases

We are learning how to:
- show that gases are matter
- show that gases have mass and occupy space.

Gases 》》

Gases are all around us, in the air. We cannot see most gases, but we can investigate their properties.

Activity 7.1

Investigating the mass of a gas

Here is what you need:

- metre rule
- string
- drawing pin
- two identical balloons.

Here is what you should do:

1. Tie three pieces of string to the metre rule: one piece hanging down from each end of the rule, and one placed exactly in the middle of the rule so that you can hold the string and balance the rule (see Fig 7.5).

2. Blow both balloons up to a good size, but do not overinflate them. They should both be blown up to the same size and a knot tied at the neck so they do not deflate.

3. Tie one balloon to the string at one end of the rule, and the other balloon to the string at the other end of the rule.

4. Hold up the string attached to the middle of the rule, so that the rule is balanced.

5. Pierce one balloon with the pin (keep hold of the pin).

6. Is the rule still balanced? What observation did you make? What conclusion can you draw?

FIG 7.5

In Activity 7.1, an equal amount of air was blown into each balloon. This explains why the metre rule was balanced. When one balloon was pierced, the air in that balloon was released. Immediately, the rule went off balance as the inflated balloon went lower. This indicates that the inflated balloon had more mass than the one with no air.

Since the inflated balloon had more mass than the pierced one, we can conclude that air must have mass.

The experiment can be repeated for gases other than air, with similar results. All gases have mass.

Activity 7.2

Investigating the volume of a gas

Here is what you need:

- trough or large flat-bottomed bowl
- water
- waterproof marker pen
- balloon.

Here is what you should do:

1. Pour water into the trough up to about half full and mark the level on the side of the trough.

2. Inflate the balloon and tie it at the neck.

3. Place the balloon gently into the trough. Does it sink?

4. Push down on the balloon. Can you make it go deeper into the water?

5. What do you observe about the water level as you push down on the balloon?

6. Can you explain what is happening?

7. Do you think that the water would behave in the same way if the balloon were filled with any other gas?

In Activity 7.2, the inflated balloon had to be pushed down into the water. The water level rose up the side of the trough as you pushed. The deeper you pushed the balloon, the higher the water level rose. This means that a greater amount of space was needed to contain both the balloon of air and the water. This is because that the air inside the balloon takes up some space. We say that the air has a **volume**.

The experiment can be repeated for any gas, not just air. All gases have volume.

Check your understanding

1. Describe how you could show that the gas oxygen has mass and volume.

2. Can you think of anything that does not have mass or volume?

> **Fun fact**
>
> All the air around us in the atmosphere has mass and volume, which means that the air is pushing down on us constantly. This is what weather forecasters mean when they talk about 'atmospheric pressure'. We are used to this pressure, so we usually do not feel it.

Key term

volume the space occupied by a three-dimensional object or substance

Density

Density »»

Density is the ratio of the mass of an object to its volume.

Activity 7.3

Investigating density

Work in groups for this activity.

Here is what you need (for each group):

- block of either wood, glass, sponge, stone or metal (each group should have a block of a different material, but of the same size, shape and volume)
- balance
- ruler.

Here is what you should do:

1. Describe your block: is it heavy or light?

2. Use the balance to find the mass of the block.

3. Use your ruler to find the volume of the block.

4. What is the ratio between the mass and the volume of your block? This is the density of the material.

5. Compare the size and mass of your group's block with the size and mass of other groups' blocks.

6. Comment on the difference in the densities of the different blocks.

a)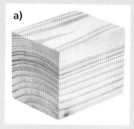

b)

e)

c)

d)

FIG 7.6 A block of **a)** wood, **b)** glass, **c)** sponge, **d)** stone, **e)** metal

The mass of a substance indicates the amount of matter of which it is made. The volume of a substance is the amount of space it occupies.

Mass should not be confused with weight. You will learn the difference between these two quantities in Topic 10.8.

When mass is divided by volume, the result tells you how heavy a volume of 1 cm³ of the substance is. The heavier 1 cm³ of the substance is, the more tightly packed are the particles that make up the substance. The more particles there are to a given volume of a substance, the more dense the substance is.

The **density** (D) of a solid is given by the ratio of its mass (m) to its volume (V), using the formula:

$$D = \frac{m}{V}$$

In this formula, mass is in grams (g) and volume in cm³. The result is the density in g/cm³.

a) lead **b)** gold **c)** aluminium **d)** potassium

FIG 7.7 Different metals have different densities: **a)** lead and **b)** gold are very dense, but **c)** aluminium and **d)** potassium are much less dense. In fact, potassium floats on water!

Check your understanding

1. The mass of a book is 500 g and its volume is 80 cm³. Find its density.

2. The volume of a block is 90 cm³ and its density is 4 g/cm³. Find its mass.

3. The density of a brick is 8 g/cm³. If its mass is 400 g, find its volume.

4. Using the information on the book, the block and the brick from questions 1, 2 and 3, place the items in ascending order based on their:

   a) mass
   b) volume
   c) density.

Fun fact

Gold is one of the densest metals that we know. Its density is 19.3 g/cm³ which is much denser than lead (density 11.3 g/cm³)

Key term

density the mass of one unit of volume of a substance; for example, 5 g per cm³ means that every cubic centimetre of the given substance has a mass of 5 grams

States of matter

We are learning how to:

- identify and differentiate between states of matter.

Matter – or stuff – is all around us. But what exactly is matter, how does it exist, and does non-matter also exist?

Activity 7.4

Classifying forms of matter

We can classify (group) things in many ways.

Here is what you should do:

1. Look at the pictures in Fig 7.8. Choose some ways of classifying the items shown. Try to be scientific.

2. What do all the things have in common?

3. What are the different features?

4. Discuss with each other the reasons for your classification.

| rain | people | soda | sun | bell | crayons |

| glue | syrup | helium | computer | rocket exhaust | lemonade |

| smoke | books | steam | milk | football | hot air |

| pear | oxygen | gasoline | hat | ice | flowers |

FIG 7.8 Examples of forms of matter

States of matter

All matter is made up of tiny units called **particles**. All matter has mass and volume. But matter exists in different forms. One way of classifying matter is by the state in which it exists. These states are: **solid**, **liquid** and **gas**.

We can determine **states of matter** by observing physical properties. Physical properties are features or characteristics that can we can observe without changing the substance.

- **Solids** have a definite volume and a **rigid** structure, which makes a definite shape.

- **Liquids** have a definite volume but no rigid structure, so they keep no definite shape. They take the shape of the part of a container that they are in.

- **Gases** have neither definite volume nor shape.

Liquids and gases are both **fluids** – they can flow – because their particles are able to easily slide over each other.

The properties of solids, liquids and gases and the arrangements of the particles in them are shown in Fig 7.9.

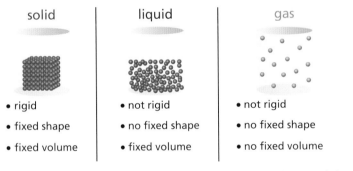

solid	liquid	gas
• rigid	• not rigid	• not rigid
• fixed shape	• no fixed shape	• no fixed shape
• fixed volume	• fixed volume	• no fixed volume

FIG 7.9 The arrangement of particles in a solid, liquid and gas, and the main properties of each state

Check your understanding

1. What properties do the following have in common:

   a) solids and liquids?
   b) liquids and gases?

2. Explain the difference between 'rigid' and 'fluid' and give examples of objects with these properties.

3. Write a description of the difference between a gas and a liquid, for someone who knows no science.

Key terms

particle a tiny bit or quantity of matter

solid the form of a substance with a rigid structure and a set volume

liquid the form of a substance with no rigid structure but a set volume

gas the form of a substance with neither a rigid structure nor a set volume

state of matter the form in which matter exists

rigid firm and set in place

fluid the form of a substance that can be continually deformed (liquid or gas)

Particles of matter

We are learning how to:

- explain that bonds between particles determine the shape and volume of each state of matter.

Particles 》》》

What determines the shape and volume of objects in different states of matter?

Activity 7.5

Investigating objects

Here is what you need:

- stones
- beaker of water
- inflated balloon
- empty bottle
- piece of wood
- sponge.
- baby powder

FIG 7.10 Materials to investigate

Here is what you should do:

1. Examine the objects. Which objects:
   a) have a fixed shape?
   b) are easily broken or separated?
   c) can be poured?
   d) can be picked up and held easily?
2. What about what is inside the balloon and the bottle?
3. List some physical properties of each object.

Bonds between particles

The tiny particles that make up matter are held together by forces called **bonds**. The way in which the particles are arranged determines whether a substance is solid, liquid or gas.

Solids can be hard like a rock, soft like fur, big like an asteroid, or powdery. Strong bonds hold the particles of solids together and make the solids tightly packed (see Fig 7.11(a)). Baby powder is made from ground-up rock (talcum powder); tiny pieces of solid can be seen in the powder, under a microscope. Solids maintain their shape and volume.

Liquids do not keep any set shape. The bonds holding the particles of a liquid together are weaker, allowing the particles to move (see Fig 7.11(b)). You cannot cut the liquid in a beaker into two pieces, because the liquid flows back to fill the space.

Gases cannot keep any shape and cannot stay in one place. Gas particles move continually, because there are almost no bonds between them (see Fig 7.11(c)). As a result, gases can take the shape of any large container and can also be **compressed** (squashed) into a tiny space.

Particles in a solid are held in position because the particles do not have enough energy to overcome the forces of attraction. Particles in a liquid move and so have more kinetic energy, but they still remain in touch with each other. Particles in a gas have much more kinetic energy, so they have sufficient energy to overcome the forces of attraction and move away from each other.

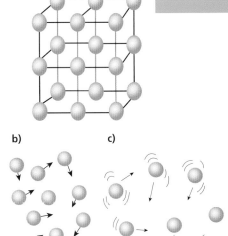

7.5

FIG 7.11 Bonds in states of matter: a) solid, b) liquid, c) gas

Check your understanding

1. Write a sentence about each of the objects you investigated in Activity 7.5. In each sentence, try to explain how the bonds between the particles of the object cause it to have an observed property. For example:

   'The stones are hard and difficult to break, because the bonds between the particles are very strong.'

   Remember that the balloon and the empty bottle are containers of gas. Think carefully about the sponge.

Key terms

bond the force of attraction between particles, holding matter together

compress squeeze into a small space

The effect of heat on matter

We are learning how to:

- explain what happens to a substance as it changes from solid to liquid and back to solid
- explain the link between the temperature and the state of matter.

Matter can melt 》》

We can investigate what happens when substances **melt**.

Activity 7.6

Room temperature – cool or warm?

Here is what you need:

- shallow dishes such as half of a Petrie dish × 4
- ice cube
- butter
- lipstick
- candle.

Here is what you should do:

1. Look at the four materials. In what state are they?

2. Place each material in a shallow dish.

3. Leave the dishes on the bench for 5 minutes.

4. Look at what has happened to each material and write down what you observe.

FIG 7.12 Experiment with melting ice

Activity 7.7

Investigating melting

Here is what you need:

- beaker of ice
- butter
- lipstick
- candle wax
- stopwatch
- tin lids × 3
- tongs
- thermometer
- cobalt chloride paper
- water bath.

Here is what you should do:

1. Place the thermometer in the beaker of ice and read its temperature.

2. Place the beaker of water above the water bath and heat it for 5 minutes. In what state is the ice now? What is its temperature?

3. Touch the ice, or what is has changed into, with the cobalt chloride paper. What colour change takes place?

4. Place a small amount of butter on a tin lid and hold it over the water bath using tongs. Using a stopwatch, time how long it takes before the butter starts to melt.

5. Repeat step 4 for the lipstick and the candle wax.

6. Which of the four materials melted quickest?

7. Which of the four materials melted slowest?

FIG 7.13 Apparatus set-up for heating tin lids

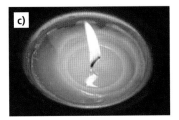

FIG 7.14 Substances melting: a) butter, b) lipstick, c) candle wax

All four materials in the Activities started as solids. At room **temperature** only the ice melted. The pink colour of the cobalt chloride paper indicated that it was just water. With a slightly warmer temperature over the water bath, the butter melted, while it took more **heat energy** to melt the candle and the wax. This shows that each substance has a different melting point. When the temperature of a substance reaches its melting point, the particles of the substance have gained enough energy to move faster and further apart. As the particles move apart, they overcome the bonds between them and they become fluid.

Each substance also has a different solidifying point. Although room temperature is high enough to melt ice, it is sufficiently cool to allow candle and wax to **solidify**. Solidifying indicates that the particles of a substance have lost enough energy to slow them down and move closer to each other. As the particles move closer, the bonds overcome the movement energy of the particles and they form a rigid structure – the substance becomes solid.

Check your understanding

1. Explain why butter can go runny in a warm room. Use the words 'melt', 'temperature', 'heat energy' and 'particles' in your explanation.

2. Explain what happens if you then put the butter in the fridge. Use the words 'temperature', 'energy', 'solidify' and 'particles' in your explanation.

Key terms

melt when a substance changes from a solid to a liquid

temperature a measure of how hot an object is

heat energy energy produced based on a change in temperature

solidify when a liquid changes form to a solid

121

Melting and solidifying

We are learning how to:

- explain that changing a substance from solid to liquid or from liquid to solid is a reversible change
- classify these changes of state as physical changes.

Reversible changes ≫

Activity 7.8

Investigating ice

When a substance changes from solid to liquid, does it remain the same substance?

Here is what you need:

- piece of cobalt chloride paper
- zip-lock bag of water.

Here is what you should do:

1. Measure the temperature of some water in a zip-lock bag. Then put it in the freezer.

2. Collect zip-lock bag from the freezer. Is the water still in the liquid state?

3. Measure the temperature and compare it with the temperature before you placed the bag in the freezer. Has it increased or decreased? Why has it?

4. Allow the ice to melt a little and then dip a piece of cobalt chloride paper into the liquid. Does it turn pink? What does that show?

5. Has melting and freezing changed the substance?

FIG 7.15 The ice in this berg is gradually melting to water

In a freezer, water exists as ice because the temperature is lower than 0 °C. When ice is exposed to room temperature, it melts because room temperature is higher than 0 °C.

At temperatures between 0 °C and 100 °C, water is in the liquid state. At any point in that range, if water is put in the freezer, the low temperature in the freezer causes the water to lose energy. Heat energy flows from the water to the inside of the freezer, causing the water to **solidify**. ('**Freezing**' is a type of 'solidification'.)

FIG 7.16 Coconut oil solidifies at low temperatures

Melting and solidification are both **changes of state**. These are **reversible** processes. The change can go either way, depending on the temperature and the flow of heat energy.

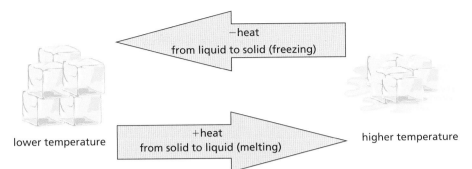

−heat
from liquid to solid (freezing)

lower temperature

+heat
from solid to liquid (melting)

higher temperature

FIG 7.17 The effect of change of temperature on melting and freezing

Neither freezing nor melting changes the composition of substances. Water remains water. Melting and solidification are **physical changes**, because the substance remains unchanged even though it goes through a change of state.

Check your understanding

1. Write down these pairs of things and draw an arrow between them to show which way the heat energy will flow. (Hint: think about what temperature they are.)

cold drink	hot sunny surroundings
hot cup of tea	normal temperature room
pie at room temperature	fridge
ice cream from freezer	normal temperature room

2. In which case in question 1 will there be a change of state?

3. Explain what we mean by a reversible change.

FIG 7.18

Key terms

solidify when a liquid changes to a solid

freezing when a substance changes from a liquid to a solid because of a change in temperature

change of state the transformation of the form of a substance

reversible the ability for a substance to return to its original form when it is transformed

physical change a transformation that does not alter the substance of the matter

Boiling and condensing

We are learning how to:

- change the state of a substance from liquid to gas and back to liquid
- explain that these are reversible changes
- classify these changes of state as physical changes.

Boiling and condensing ›››

When a liquid is heated it will eventually reach its boiling point and become a gas or vapour. When a gas is cooled it turns back into a liquid.

If you leave a cold bottle of drink on a table, it soon gets wet on the outside. The air near the bottle, which contains water **vapour**, has been cooled by the bottle. This causes the vapour to condense, forming liquid drops of water on the outside of the bottle.

Activity 7.9

Investigating boiling and condensation

Is the change from liquid to gas a change of substance?

Here is what you need:

- Bunsen burner
- distillation apparatus
- conical flask.

Here is what you should do:

1. Set up the apparatus as shown in Fig 7.19.
2. Place some water in the flask that is above the Bunsen burner.
3. Heat the flask of water until the water boils, and observe what happens.
4. What happens in the conical flask?
5. After a few minutes, turn off the Bunsen burner and allow the apparatus to cool down. Then, dip a piece of cobalt chloride paper into the liquid in the conical flask. Does it turn pink? What does that show?
6. Is this what you expected? Has the water changed?

As water is heated, the increase in temperature causes the particles to gain energy and move further apart. As the particles move faster and further apart, they overcome the bonds between them and the bonds eventually break.

Water becomes a gas when the bonds between its particles no longer exist. This is called **boiling**. The change from liquid to gas can be described as **vaporisation**.

When we cool a gas, heat energy flows from it. The loss of heat energy causes the particles to slow down, and the bonds between them begin to exert an effect. The particles move closer together. The gas changes to a liquid. This is **condensing**. Another word to describe this change is **liquefaction**.

Boiling and condensing are reversible, depending on the direction of flow of heat energy.

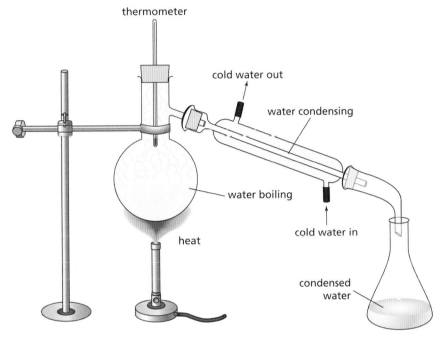

FIG 7.19 Apparatus set-up for boiling and condensing

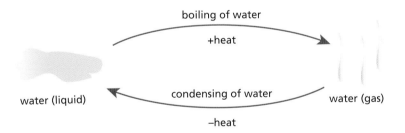

FIG 7.20 Heat energy flow, boiling and condensing

The change from liquid to gas and back did not change the substance of the water. This means that these changes of state are both physical changes.

Check your understanding

1. Draw a flow chart to show what happens to boiling water leaving a kettle and condensing on cold tiles behind a hob. Make sure you use the words 'boil', 'temperature', 'condense' and 'heat energy'.

Key terms

vapour another term to describe a gas

boiling the process by which a liquid changes to a gas at its boiling point

vaporisation when a substances changes to a gas

condensing when a gas changes to a liquid

liquefaction when either a solid or a gas changes to a liquid

Evaporation

Evaporation »»

If we leave a glass of water on a sunny window ledge the water will soon 'disappear', leaving an empty glass. The water changes to gas and is lost to the atmosphere.

Although the sun's rays may be hot they will certainly not heat the water to 100 °C so the water in the glass does not boil. Clearly there must be another process by which a liquid can change into a gas.

The particles in a liquid are in continual motion and have different amounts of kinetic energy. At any given time a very small proportion of particles at the surface of the liquid have sufficient energy to move away from the rest and become gas. This process is called **evaporation**.

Evaporation is the process by which a liquid becomes a gas or vapour at temperatures below its boiling point. The term '**vapour**' is often used to describe a gas below the boiling point of the liquid from which it has formed. Thus when water evaporates it may be said to form water vapour rather than steam.

There are two important differences between evaporation and boiling.

- A substance only boils at a particular temperature, called its boiling point. Evaporation takes place at any temperature but is greatest in warm, moving air.

- Evaporation only takes place at the surface of a liquid while boiling takes place throughout the liquid.

Although evaporation takes place below the boiling point of a liquid, energy is still needed to convert a liquid to a vapour. When a liquid evaporates, therefore, it absorbs energy.

FIG 7.21 Evaporation takes place at any temperature

Activity 7.10

Showing that evaporation requires energy

Here is what you will need:

- a few drops of a volatile liquid like ethoxyethane.

Here is what you should do:

1. Place a few drops of a volatile liquid on the back of your hand.

2. Hold your hand still and allow the liquid to evaporate.

3. What sensation do you feel on your skin?

4. What does this tell you about evaporation?

Volatile liquids are liquids which have low boiling points and evaporate very quickly.

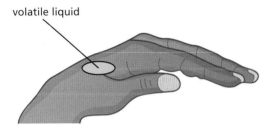

FIG 7.22 Cooling effect of evaporation

If a small amount of a volatile liquid, such as ethoxyethane, is placed on the back of the hand, it will evaporate so quickly that the skin where the liquid was will feel cold. The heat energy needed for evaporation is taken from the skin.

Check your understanding

1. Fig 7.24 shows a simple way of keeping soda cool on a warm day. A bottle of soda is wrapped in a wet towel and hung on a washing line in the breeze.

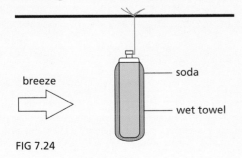

FIG 7.24

Explain how this works.

Key terms

evaporation the process by which a liquid changes to a gaseous state below its boiling point

volatile the property of quickly changing from liquid to gas at room temperature

vapour another term for a gas

Sublimation

We are learning how to:

- define sublimation and desublimation
- explain why sublimation and desublimation are physical changes.

Sublimation »

We know that when heated a solid can change to a liquid, and when heated further a liquid can change to a gas. Do all substances go through the liquid state when they change from solid to gas?

Activity 7.11

Observing sublimation

Here is what you need:

- crystal of iodine
- test tube
- cotton wool
- water bath
- beaker of iced water.

Here is what you should do:

1. Place a single crystal of iodine in the bottom of a test tube. Seal the tube with a cotton wool plug.

2. Warm the test tube gently in a hot water bath.

3. Observe the iodine vapour that fills the test tube.

4. Cool the test tube in iced water.

5. Discuss the following:

   a) What does heat do to iodine?

   b) Is any liquid present?

   c) Where do the fumes go?

   d) What happens to the fumes? Why does this happen?

   e) Can you tell whether the change is a physical one?

a) b)

FIG 7.25 **a)** Iodine being heated; **b)** gaseous iodine cooling

Some substances change directly from their solid state to their gaseous state when heat energy is applied. As soon as the heat energy is withdrawn, they return to the solid state. These processes are referred to as **sublimation** and **desublimation**.

Sublimation and desublimation are both physical changes – the substance, such as the iodine in Activity 7.11, remains unchanged. Another example of a solid that sublimes is **dry ice** (Fig 7.26).

FIG 7.26 Dry ice subliming

Dry ice is the solid form of carbon dioxide. It is used as a cooling agent. Dry ice has two advantages in that its temperature is lower than that of water ice and it leaves no residue. It is used for preserving frozen foods such as ice cream. The extreme cold of dry ice makes it dangerous to handle. Direct contact with dry ice can cause severe burns.

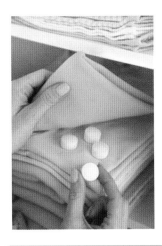

FIG 7.28 Moth balls are made of naphthalene, which sublimes at room temperature. The naphthalene vapour that is given off is harmful to insects, so it can keep clothes free from insect pests

Fun fact

FIG 7.27

Because solid carbon dioxide sublimes at room temperature, it is often used at concerts or in plays where the effect of fog or smoke is required. The cold carbon dioxide condenses the water vapour in the air and creates clouds of water droplets.

Key terms

sublimation the change from a solid to a gas without liquefaction

desublimation the change from a gas to a solid without liquefaction

dry ice the solid form of carbon dioxide

Check your understanding

1. Is heating needed for sublimation?

2. Draw a diagram, like those in Figs 7.17 and 7.20, to show the sublimation and desublimation of a substance.

Measuring the freezing points of vegetable oils

Ms Dinnal bought a bottle of coconut oil to use in her cooking. She placed it in her refrigerator overnight. The next morning she was surprised to find that it had become solid and she could no longer pour it from the bottle.

If the manufacturer had given the freezing point of coconut oil on the bottle this problem might have been avoided. Information about the freezing points of different vegetable oils would help people to decide the best ways of storing them.

FIG 7.29 Oils become solids when cooled

1. You are going to work in a group of four to investigate the freezing points of different oils commonly used in food preparation. The tasks are:

   - to find out what vegetable oils are available from your local stores
   - to devise a method of measuring the freezing points of vegetable oils
   - to measure the freezing points of different vegetable oils
   - to ensure the values you obtain are accurate
   - to prepare an information sheet that provides useful advice about the storage of different vegetable oils.

a) Have a look at the different vegetable oils available in your local shops. Here are some you might see:

   olive oil   soybean oil   corn oil   sunflower oil
   coconut oil   palm kernel oil   peanut oil

   Are all of these available? Are there any other vegetable oils not on this list?

   You will need to obtain a small quantity of each of the oils available for the investigation you are going to carry out.

b) How are you going to find the freezing point of a vegetable oil? This is when it changes from liquid vegetable oil to solid vegetable oil or fat.

   For any particular vegetable oil the freezing point of the liquid oil is the same as the melting point of the solid fat. Perhaps it would be easier to find the temperature at which the fat melts?

   All of the oils mentioned above have melting points in the range −20 °C to 25 °C.

FIG 7.30 Freezer and fridge temperatures

A typical refrigerator cools to 5 °C and a typical freezer cools to –20 °C. Does this give you any idea how you might convert a liquid oil to a solid fat?

How are you going to measure the melting point of a fat? It isn't easy to insert a thermometer into the fat. Perhaps you could allow a liquid oil to solidify into a fat with a thermometer already inserted in it?

One method of finding the melting point of a solid oil is to gently warm a test tube of the solid in water at room temperature. You might be able to suggest a different way.

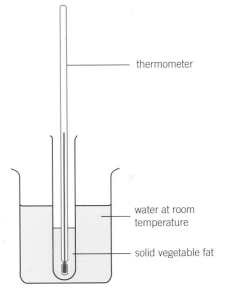

FIG 7.31 One way of measuring melting point

c) A good scientific method should be repeatable and provide consistent results.

How often will you repeat your procedure for each vegetable oil to ensure your answers are as accurate as possible?

d) Construct an information sheet that can be used to guide people about the storage of vegetable oils. You might simply give a list of vegetable oils and their melting points or you might be more ambitious and include some illustrations and advice on storage.

e) Give an oral presentation to the class on what you found out about the freezing points of different vegetable oils. This should include a demonstration of how you obtained your data.

Unit 8: Atoms and elements

We are learning how to:

- explain that matter is made of elements.

Matter's building blocks ⟫

As we have seen previously, all matter is made of particles. Pure substances are made of only one kind of particle. The simplest particles are called atoms and these are particles that cannot be broken down. Substances made of similar atoms are called elements.

Elements

An **element** is a single substance that cannot be split into simpler substances. Fig 8.1 shows a range of elements with which you may be familiar.

Every element is unique. Scientists have given each element a unique name, a unique set of letters as an identifying **symbol**, and a unique number.

There are 118 elements which have been identified and arranged into a chart called the **Periodic Table**, as shown in Fig 8.2.

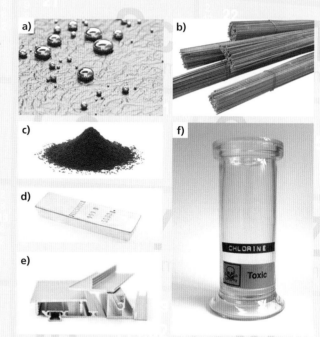

FIG 8.1 Elements you may already know about include **a)** mercury, **b)** iron, **c)** carbon, **d)** silver, **e)** aluminium and **f)** chlorine

1 H Hydrogen																	2 He Helium
3 Li Lithium	4 Be Beryllium											5 B Boron	6 C Carbon	7 N Nitrogen	8 O Oxygen	9 F Fluorine	10 Ne Neon
11 Na Sodium	12 Mg Magnesium											13 Al Aluminium	14 Si Silicon	15 P Phosphorus	16 S Sulfur	17 Cl Chlorine	18 Ar Argon
19 K Potassium	20 Ca Calcium	21 Sc Scandium	22 Ti Titanium	23 V Vanadium	24 Cr Chromium	25 Mn Manganese	26 Fe Iron	27 Co Cobalt	28 Ni Nickel	29 Cu Copper	30 Zn Zinc	31 Ga Gallium	32 Ge Germanium	33 As Arsenic	34 Se Selenium	35 Br Bromine	36 Kr Krypton
37 Rb Rubidium	38 Sr Strontium	39 Y Yttrium	40 Zr Zirconium	41 Nb Niobium	42 Mo Molybdenum	43 Tc Technetium	44 Ru Ruthenium	45 Rh Rhodium	46 Pd Palladium	47 Ag Silver	48 Cd Cadmium	49 In Indium	50 Sn Tin	51 Sb Antimony	52 Te Tellurium	53 I Iodine	54 Xe Xenon
55 Cs Caesium	56 Ba Barium	57-71 Lanthanide	72 Hf Hafnium	73 Ta Tantalum	74 W Tungsten	75 Re Rhenium	76 Os Osmium	77 Ir Iridium	78 Pt Platinum	79 Au Gold	80 Hg Mercury	81 Tl Thallium	82 Pb Lead	83 Bi Bismuth	84 Po Polonium	85 At Astatine	86 Rn Radon
87 Fr Francium	88 Ra Radium	89-103 Actinides	104 Rf Rutherfordium	105 Db Dubnium	106 Sg Seaborgium	107 Bh Bohrium	108 Hs Hassium	109 Mt Meitnerium	110 Ds Darmstadtium	111 Rg Roentgenium	112 Cn Copernicium	113 Uut Ununtrium	114 Fl Flerovium	115 Uup Ununpentium	116 Lv Livermorium	117 Uus Ununseptium	118 Uuo Ununoctium

57 La Lanthanum	58 Ce Cerium	59 Pr Praseodymium	60 Nd Neodymium	61 Pm Promethium	62 Sm Samarium	63 Eu Europium	64 Gd Gadolinium	65 Tb Terbium	66 Dy Dysprosium	67 Ho Holmium	68 Er Erbium	69 Tm Thulium	70 Yb Ytterbium	71 Lu Lutetium
89 Ac Actinium	90 Th Thorium	91 Pa Protactinium	92 U Uranium	93 Np Neptunium	94 Pu Plutonium	95 Am Americium	96 Cm Curium	97 Bk Berkelium	98 Cf Californium	99 Es Einsteinium	100 Fm Fermium	101 Md Mendelevium	102 No Nobelium	103 Lr Lawrencium

FIG 8.2 The Periodic Table

Looking at the arrangement of elements

Here is what you should do:

1. Look again at the Periodic Table in Fig 8.2.

    a) How have the elements been arranged?

    b) Is there an order to the numbering?

The Periodic Table is arranged into rows and columns. The elements in each column share common characteristics. Also, all elements with the same colour in the chart share similar features.

The number shown at the top left in each box is the **atomic number** of that element.

The symbol for each element consists of one, two or (rarely) three letters; only the first is capitalised. The symbol for each element was taken from the element's original name in Swedish, Latin, French or German. For example, sodium is Na from Natrium and lead is Pb from Plumbum, both of which are Latin. The symbol for Tungsten is W from Wolfram, which is Swedish.

> **Fun fact**
>
> The letters 'J' and 'Q' are the only ones that do not appear in the full Periodic Table.

Check your understanding

1. How is an 'element' defined?

2. What is the atomic number of:

    a) boron?

    b) magnesium?

    c) lithium?

    d) aluminium?

    e) argon?

3. What are the atomic symbols for:

    a) chlorine?

    b) potassium?

    c) helium?

    d) calcium?

    e) nitrogen?

4. How were the symbols for each element chosen?

> **Key terms**
>
> **element** a single substance that cannot be split into simpler substances
>
> **symbol** letters used to stand for the full name of an element
>
> **Periodic Table** a harmonious arrangement of the 118 known elements despite their varied characteristics
>
> **atomic number** the number of protons in the nucleus of an atom; this number determines the place of each element in the Periodic Table

Some common elements

We are learning how to:

- describe some elements
- give the common uses of some elements.

Elements ▶▶▶

Some materials that we use contain only one element. For example, an aluminium pan contains only the element aluminium.

FIG 8.3 This pan is made of the element aluminium

Table 8.1 gives some information about some common elements.

Element	Uses and/or description
aluminium	a light metal used in making airplanes, buildings, pots and pans
bromine	used to make chemicals, and in photography, medicines and insecticides
calcium	a soft metal present in chemicals that form limestone, marble and chalk
carbon	found in coal, oil, gas, living things and inks
copper	a metal used for electric wires, pots, pans and small coins
hydrogen	a flammable and explosive gas
iodine	used on cuts and wounds to kill germs
manganese	a metal used with other metals to form alloys
mercury	a heavy, poisonous liquid used in some thermometers
neon	a gas used in many lights and signs
potassium	present in fertilisers
radon	used in earthquake prediction
sulfur	used to make sulfuric acid and some medicines, such as pet anti-flea powders
titanium	a metal used to form alloys with aluminium
uranium	a metal used in some nuclear reactors

TABLE 8.1 Information about some elements

Fun fact

The foods that we eat are sources of elements which are good for our growth, repair and general wellbeing. Examples of some foods and their nutritional elements are:

- milk – calcium
- bananas – potassium
- fish – iodine
- eggs – sulfur.

FIG 8.4 Bananas contain traces of the element potassium

Learning about the first 20 elements

Here is what you should do:

1. Learn the first 20 elements and their symbols.

Although there are over 100 elements, you only need to commit to memory the name, symbol and number of the first 20 elements. A section of the Periodic Table showing the first 20 elements is given in Fig 8.5 below.

1 H Hydrogen									2 He Helium
3 Li Lithium	4 Be Beryllium	5 B Boron	6 C Carbon	7 N Nitrogen	8 O Oxygen	9 F Fluorine			10 Ne Neon
11 Na Sodium	12 Mg Magnesium	13 Al Aluminium	14 Si Silicon	15 P Phosphorus	16 S Sulfur	17 Cl Chlorine			18 Ar Argon
19 K Potassium	20 Ca Calcium								

FIG 8.5 The first 20 elements of the Periodic Table

Check your understanding

1. Look at the list of the first 20 elements in the Periodic Table in Fig 8.5. Pick out the elements that are not mentioned in Table 8.1, and draw up a table to show:

   a) their names and symbols

   b) what the elements are like and what they are used for – to find out, do some research on the internet.

2. Why do you think that water cannot be found in the Periodic Table?

Atoms

We are learning how to:

- define what an atom is
- sketch a diagram of an atom.

Elements and atoms ▶▶▶

An element is a substance that cannot be split into simpler substances. Elements are made up of **atoms**, all of the same type.

The idea of small units of matter called atoms was first proposed around 600 BC by a Greek called Democritus. However, for the next 2000 years, both the word and the idea disappeared. About 200 years ago, the scientist John Dalton developed, from his experiments, a theory of atomic matter. Dalton's basic theory is still used today, although much more research was needed to discover the nature of the atom itself.

Atoms are too small to see, so we need models to visualise them.

Atoms are defined as the tiniest indivisible part of an element that can exist on its own. An atom of gold is the smallest piece of gold we can get.

Each atom consists of three types of particles: protons, neutrons and electrons. These three particles are referred to as **subatomic particles**. At the centre of every atom is a nucleus, containing the protons and neutrons. The electrons orbit the nucleus in ring-like structures called shells or orbits.

FIG 8.6 The chemist John Dalton who lived from 1766 to 1844

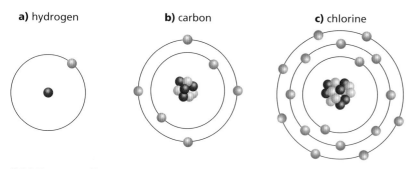

a) hydrogen   **b)** carbon   **c)** chlorine

FIG 8.7 Atoms of hydrogen, carbon and chlorine

Atomic number

The number that each element has in the Periodic Table (Fig 8.2) is based on the characteristics of the atoms that make up the element. This number is called the **atomic number** of the element. The atomic number is the number of protons in the nucleus of each atom of that element.

The atomic number (Z) is the number of protons (p), and this is equal to the number of electrons (e) that each atom of the element has; that is:

$$Z = \text{number of p} = \text{number of e}$$

Activity 8.3

Here is what you should do:

1. Copy and complete the following table. Refer to the Periodic Table in Fig 8.2.

Element/ atom	Symbol	Atomic number Z	No. of p	No. of e
magnesium				
	Ar			
		5		
			13	
				9
			19	
		2		
	S			
chlorine				

TABLE 8.2

2. Compare your responses with those of your group members.

Fun fact

A single glass of water contains more atoms than the oceans of the Earth contain glasses of water.

FIG 8.8

Check your understanding

1. How many electrons will orbit atoms of:

   a) neon?
   b) lithium?
   c) magnesium?
   d) calcium?
   e) phosphorus?

2. On a large piece of paper, draw your own diagram of an atom of:

   a) helium
   b) silicon
   c) sodium
   d) argon
   e) boron.

Key terms

atom the smallest indivisible part of an element that can exist on its own

subatomic particle particles found within an atom

atomic number the number of protons in the nucleus of an atom; this number determines the place of each element in the Periodic Table

Structure of an atom

We are learning how to:

- name subatomic particles and state their charges
- state the number of protons, neutrons and electrons in a given atom
- explain why an atom has no charge.

Atoms >>>

An atom consists of three types of subatomic particle: **protons**, **neutrons** and **electrons**.

At the centre of every atom is its **nucleus**, containing the protons and neutrons.

The electrons move around the nucleus in **shells** or **orbits**.

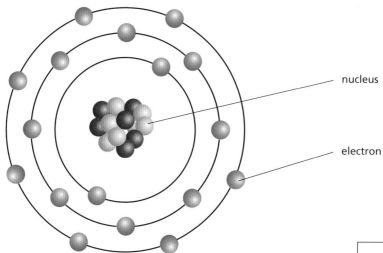

nucleus

electron

FIG 8.9 The subatomic particles in an atom

Protons and electrons are electrically charged. Neutrons are neutral – they have no electric charge. Table 8.3 summarises these charges.

An atom carries an equal number of positive and negative particles and is, therefore, neutral.

Particle	Charge
proton (p)	+1
neutron (n)	0
electron (e)	−1

TABLE 8.3 Charges of particles in atoms

Mass number

Sometimes, a Periodic Table shows two numbers for each element. The smaller number is the atomic number, and the larger number is the **mass number**.

The mass number (M) is the sum of the number of protons and neutrons (n) that are in the nucleus of an atom of the element; that is:

$$M = \text{number of p} + \text{number of n}$$

atomic number

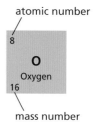

8

O

Oxygen

16

mass number

FIG 8.10 Elements have an atomic number and a mass number

1							2
H Hydrogen 1							**He** Helium 4
3	4	5	6	7	8	9	10
Li Lithium 7	**Be** Beryllium 9	**B** Boron 11	**C** Carbon 12	**N** Nitrogen 14	**O** Oxygen 16	**F** Fluorine 19	**Ne** Neon 20
11	12	13	14	15	16	17	18
Na Sodium 23	**Mg** Magnesium 24	**Al** Aluminium 27	**Si** Silicon 28	**P** Phosphorus 31	**S** Sulfur 32	**Cl** Chlorine 35	**Ar** Argon 40
19	20						
K Potassium 39	**Ca** Calcium 40						

FIG 8 11 The first 20 elements in the Periodic Table, including mass numbers

Activity 8.4

Here is what you should do:

Copy and complete the following table.

Element/ atom	Symbol	Atomic number Z	No. of p	No. of e	No. of n	Mass number M
lithium						7
	Ar					40
			17	18		
calcium		20				
		6				12
	Na				12	

TABLE 8.4

Compare your responses with those of your group members.

Check your understanding

1. State the value of the charge of each of the following particles:

   a) electron   **b)** proton   **c)** neutron.

2. Hydrogen has $Z = 1$ and $M = 1$.

   a) What particles does the atom have?

   b) Is an atom of hydrogen neutral?

Key terms

proton the subatomic particle carrying a positive electrical charge

neutron the subatomic particle carrying no electrical charge

electron the subatomic particle carrying a negative electrical charge

nucleus the centre of an atom, which may contain protons and neutrons

shell a ring-like structure formed by the arrangement of electrons around the nucleus

orbit a ring-like structure around the nucleus, containing electrons

mass number the total number of protons and neutrons that are in the nucleus of an atom of an element

Electronic structure

We are learning how to:

- write the electronic configuration of atoms in numerical form
- draw the electronic configuration of atoms.

Electronic structure »

Electron shells

The electrons orbiting the nucleus of an atom move in shells. The innermost shell can only contain two electrons. Helium has just two electrons orbiting in a single electron shell. Lithium is the next element in the Periodic Table and it has three electrons. The third electron has to orbit in a second electron shell all on its own. (see Fig 8.12).

The second electron shell can hold up to eight electrons. Neon, with ten electrons in all, has two in its inner shell and eight in its outer shell. The next element after neon is sodium. Its eleventh electron has to become the first electron in a third electron shell. The third electron shell can also hold up to eight electrons.

The term **electronic configuration** means the arrangement of the electrons of the atom.

a) helium   **b)** lithium

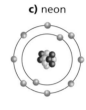

c) neon   **d)** sodium

FIG 8.12

Activity 8.5

1. Fill in the table below.

Atom	Atomic number	Number of shells
chlorine		
helium		
potassium		
lithium		
calcium		
neon		
magnesium		

TABLE 8.5

2. Draw the atomic structure of:

   a) nitrogen

   b) magnesium

   c) argon

   d) silicon.

Key term

electronic configuration the arrangement of electrons in an atom

The written electronic configuration is a shorter way of showing the arrangement of electrons of any atom.

Atom	Li	Be	B	C	N	O	F	Ne
Electronic configuration	2,1	2,2	2,3	2,4	2,5	2,6	2,7	2,8

TABLE 8.6 Written electronic configuration of atoms

Activity 8.6

Drawing and writing the electronic configuration of atoms

Here is what you should do:

1. Using the same method as in Activity 8.5, complete electronic configuration drawings for all the other elements in your chart.

   Remember the rules:

   • the first shell can have no more than two electrons

   • the second shell can have no more than eight electrons

   • the third shell can have no more than eight electrons.

2. Now write the numerical configurations for each element. Remember that these are written starting with the number of electrons on the innermost shell.

The atoms of helium, neon and argon have full outer electron shells. This means they are very stable elements and do not react or burn easily. They can be used in lighting tubes as they are unreactive.

Check your understanding

1. What is the numerical electronic configuration of hydrogen?

2. Copy Table 8.6 and add a row for the next eight elements. Complete this row. What do you notice?

3. On your completed chart of electronic configurations, look at the outer shells of the atoms of elements in the right-hand column. What do you notice?

a) helium

b) neon

c) argon

d) krypton

e) xenon

FIG 8.13 The noble gases are found in the right-hand column of the Periodic Table. Their electronic configurations mean they are stable elements, so they are used in lighting for many different purposes

A closer look at the Periodic Table

We are learning how to:

- position elements in the Periodic Table.

Elements in the Periodic Table ▶▶▶

Each element has its own unique, fixed position in the Periodic Table.

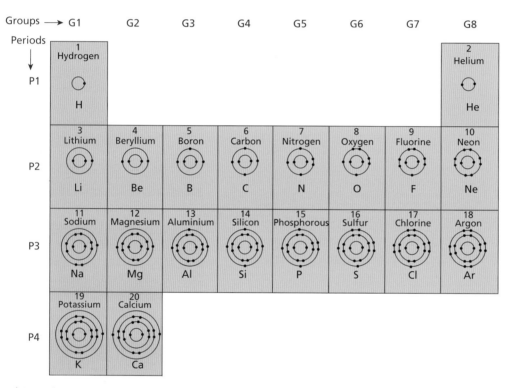

FIG 8.14 Element positions in the Periodic Table

The unique position of each element in the Periodic Table is based on its period and group. We count the number of rows down as the **period number**, and the number of columns across as the **group number**. The position of oxygen is Period 2, Group 6 written as P2, G6. The element in P3, G5 is phosphorus.

Activity 8.7

Study Fig 8.14 to answer the following questions.

1. Identify the element in the following positions (P, period; G, group):

   a) P2, G3   **b)** P3, G4   **c)** P1, G1

   d) P2, G5   **e)** P3, G8.

2. Give the position of the following elements with respect to period (P) and group (G):

   a) magnesium   **b)** lithium   **c)** sulfur

   d) beryllium   **e)** calcium.

Groups and periods

The group number and period number give more information than just the position of each element. They also provide some data concerning the structure of each atom.

The number of shells in an atom is the same as its period number.

As you move along the period, the group changes. The number of electrons in the outermost shell of any atom is the same as its group number.

Check your understanding

1. How is an 'element' defined?

   a) An atom has three shells. Which period of the Periodic Table is it in?

   b) What else do you need to know to fully describe the atom?

2. Refer to Fig 8.13 and complete the table below.

Atom	Atomic number	Number of shells	Number of electrons in outermost shell
F			
Al			
N			
Ca			
Si			

TABLE 8.7

Key terms

period number the row of the Periodic Table in which an element is found

group number the column of the Periodic Table in which an element is found

Unit 9: Compounds and mixtures

We are learning how to:

- Identify the differences between mixtures and compounds.

The difference between mixtures and compounds ⟩⟩

Elements can be mixed to form **mixtures** or combined to form **compounds**. What is the difference?

A mixture contains a number of substances together, such as rice and salt, which can be separated quite easily. Can you say how you could separate a mixture of rice and salt?

A compound is a substance that cannot be separated easily. Salt is a compound of sodium and chlorine, but it is very difficult to get back to the sodium metal and the chlorine gas.

Activity 9.1

Making mixtures and compounds

You will need:

- iron filings
- sulfur
- filter paper
- magnet.

Here is what you should do:

1. Place a small amount of iron filings on one sheet of filter paper and a little sulfur on another.

2. Place the magnet under each sheet and observe the substances.

3. Combine the two elements on a piece of filter paper. Is each one easily identifiable?

4. Place the magnet under the paper. What do you observe?

5. Is it possible to separate the two substances using the magnet? Do not use the magnet above the substances, only below the paper. (It is almost impossible to remove iron filings from a magnet.)

We can also combine iron and sulfur by heating them together in a crucible. This creates a new substance called iron sulfide.

FIG 9.1 Mixing iron and sulfur

Iron and sulfur are both elements. The grey iron filings are metallic and magnetic. Sulfur is a yellow powder.

In Activity 9.1 iron and sulfur were simply mixed together and it was easy to separate them by physical means using a magnet. No new substance was formed because no **chemical reaction** took place.

Chemical bonding and compounds

When the mixture of iron and sulfur is heated a chemical reaction takes place. **Chemical bonds** form between the atoms of iron and those of sulfur. A new substance called iron sulfide is formed.

FIG 9.2 Heating iron and sulfur

iron + sulfur $\longrightarrow$ iron sulfide

$$Fe + S \longrightarrow FeS$$

It is not possible to separate the iron and sulfur in iron sulfide with a magnet. Iron sulfide is a compound of iron and sulfur. It has different properties from both iron and sulfur.

The differences between mixtures and compounds are given in Table 9.1.

Mixture	Compound
The composition of a mixture can vary.	The composition of a compound is fixed and cannot vary.
The physical properties of a mixture are an average of its components.	A compound has its own physical properties.
The chemical properties of a mixture are a combination of its components.	A compound has its own chemical properties.
Mixing is a physical process and involves no chemical reaction.	When a compound is formed a chemical reaction takes place and bonds are broken and formed.
Mixtures can be separated by physical processes.	Compounds cannot be broken down by physical processes.

TABLE 9.1 Differences between mixtures and compounds

1. Give one piece of evidence that indicates when a sulfur and iron mixture changes to a compound.

2. Why is it possible, with a magnet, to separate iron and sulfur in a mixture, but not in iron sulfide?

Key terms

mixture a combination of two or more substances in which each substance retains its own chemical properties

compound a substance in which atoms of two or more elements are held together by chemical bonds

chemical reaction a process in which bonds form between particles of different elements

chemical bond forces by which particles of different elements are held together in a chemical compound

Atoms and molecules

We are learning how to:

- represent the atoms of a molecule
- work out the number of atoms in a molecule.

Molecules 〉〉〉

A **molecule** is a group of atoms **bonded** together. Some elements are made up of atoms bonded together – oxygen gas consists of molecules with two atoms of oxygen bonded together.

Compounds may also be made up of molecules. Water, for example, is not an element – it is a compound of hydrogen and oxygen. A water molecule has two hydrogen atoms bonded to a single oxygen atom.

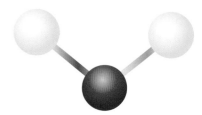

FIG 9.3 A water molecule

Activity 9.2

Here is what you should do:

1. Discuss these points in your group.

   a) What are elements made up of?

   b) When a chemical equation is written, such as
   $$Fe + S \longrightarrow FeS$$
   what is represented by the Fe and the S?

   c) What do you think is happening to the atoms in this equation?

   d) How many atoms of Fe and how many of S were used to make FeS?

iron sulphide

FIG 9.4 Iron sulfide

Drawing models of molecules

We can represent molecules using models and diagrams. Simple ball shapes are used for the atoms and, since there are bonds between the atoms, sticks or lines are used for these.

Fig 9.5 shows how we represent molecules of water (H_2O), carbon dioxide (CO_2), ammonia (NH_3) and methane (CH_4).

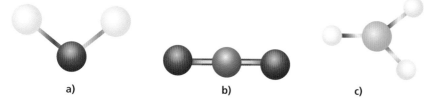

a)   b)   c)   d)

FIG 9.5 Models of molecules: **a)** H_2O, **b)** CO_2, **c)** NH_3 and **d)** CH_4

FIG 9.6 A bottle of white vinegar; vinegar is ethanoic acid, which is made of molecules of carbon, hydrogen and oxygen, $C_2H_4O_2$

How many atoms make a molecule?

Each molecule is made up of a specific number of atoms. The **formula** for water is H_2O. This shows that it takes two atoms of hydrogen (H) and one atom of oxygen (O) to make one molecule of water. A water molecule consists of three atoms.

Vinegar, for example, is mostly ethanoic acid. Ethanoic acid has the formula $C_2H_4O_2$. This means that each molecule of ethanoic acid is made up of two atoms of carbon, four atoms of hydrogen and two atoms of oxygen.

Some compounds have many atoms.

Check your understanding

1. Look at the models in Fig 9.5. Copy them and label them. Which colour ball is used for:

   a) oxygen (O)?

   b) hydrogen (H)?

   c) carbon (C)?

2. Identify the number of atoms in the molecules with the following formulas:

   a) CO_2

   b) NH_3

   c) SO_2

   d) PCl_5

   e) N_2O_5

   f) C_2H_6O.

Key terms

molecule one unit of a compound

bonded chemically connected

formula a symbolic representation of the atoms within one molecule of a substance

Molecules that are elements

We are learning how to:

- explain that not only compounds are made up of molecules
- define 'polyatomic'
- explain why diamond is not polyatomic.

Diatomic and polyatomic molecules »»

Molecules are not always made of different atoms. Sometimes they are made of only one type of atom. In other words, an element can exist as a molecule.

Some gases are made up of pairs of identical atoms, bonded together as a molecule. Because two atoms are bonded together to form each molecule of the gas, the gas is referred to as a **diatomic** gas.

Since the molecule is made of only one type of atom, it is an element, not a compound. Oxygen gas is one such example. Oxygen gas is always written O_2, not just O. Its molecular model is shown in Fig 9.7.

FIG 9.7 A molecule of the element oxygen

There are other elements that exist as **polyatomic** molecules, such as phosphorus and sulfur (Fig 9.8).

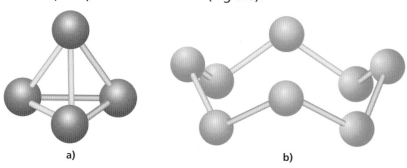

FIG 9.8 Polyatomic molecules: a) phosphorus, b) sulfur

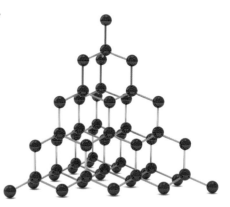

FIG 9.9 The structure of diamond

A polyatomic molecule is a single unit formed of at least three atoms.

Diamond is a precious stone that consists of a clear and colourless crystalline form of pure carbon. In diamond, the carbon atoms are all bonded to each other in a crystal structure that can be very large. This is called a macromolecule.

Carbon

Carbon has the ability to form different kinds of substances. We have seen the structure of diamond on the previous page. See if you can research more about other forms of carbon, such as 'buckyballs' and the carbon tubes used in nanotechnology.

a)

b)

c)

d)
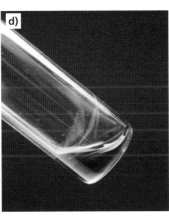

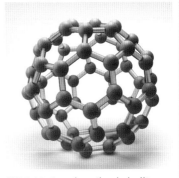
FIG 9.10 Carbon is an element that comes in several forms: **a)** plain carbon made of individual carbon atoms; **b)** graphite made of sheets of carbon atoms bonded together; **c)** diamond, made of large polyatomic molecules; and **d)** buckminsterfullerene, which is a molecule made up of 60 carbon atoms

Key terms

diatomic describes a molecule with two atoms only

polyatomic describes a molecule containing many atoms

Check your understanding

1. Write the formulas for the following diatomic gases:

   a) nitrogen
   b) hydrogen
   c) chlorine.

2. Draw a molecular model for hydrogen. Look back to Fig 9.5 to see which colour you should use.

3. What does 'polyatomic' mean?

4. Find out about carbon 'buckyballs'. Why are they called 'buckyballs'?

Review of Matter and particles

Properties of matter

- All matter has mass and volume.
- The ratio of mass to volume for a substance is called its density.
- Different types of matter have different densities.
- We can find the density of an object or a substance by experiment.
- Matter exists in different forms, called states.
- States of matter can be determined by physical properties:
  - solids have definite volume and shape
  - liquids have definite volume but no definite shape
  - gases have neither definite volume nor shape.
- All matter is composed of tiny particles held together by bonds.
- The particles in any substance remain the same. However, both the energy of the substance and the arrangement of its particles can change. These two changes determine whether a substance is solid, liquid or gas.
- The particles of a solid are held together by strong bonds, which makes them tightly packed. They cannot be compressed. The particles have little energy.
- Liquids do not keep any set shape. They flow. The bonds holding the particles of a liquid together are very weak, but the particles cannot be compressed. The particles have energy and move about.
- Gases do not keep any shape. They can take the shape of any large container and can be compressed. The particles have a lot of energy and move about freely and quickly.
- When the temperature of a solid is increased, its particles gain energy. The solid may change to a liquid and then to a gas as the particles move faster and further apart.
- When the temperature is decreased, the processes are reversed.
- Melting, boiling, condensing and freezing are all physical changes, since they do not change the composition of the substance. All these processes occur in nature, for example in the water cycle.
- Some substances sublime, that is they change directly from solid to gas. Desublimation is the reverse process. Both sublimation and desublimation are physical changes.
- Dry ice is the solid form of carbon dioxide. It is used as a cooling and preserving agent. It sublimes, so it is also used to create 'fog' effects.

Atomic structure

- The idea of atoms of matter was first proposed around 600 BC, but resurfaced about 200 years ago when Dalton developed an atomic theory, which is still being used today.
- An atom is the smallest indivisible part of an element that can exist on its own.
- An atom consists of protons, neutrons and electrons.

- The nucleus at the centre of the atom contains the protons and neutrons.
- The electrons orbit in shells around the nucleus.
- The atomic number (Z), the number of protons (p) and the number of electrons (e) are equal.
- The mass number (M) is the sum of the number of protons (p) and the number of neutrons (n).
- Protons have one positive electric charge, electrons have one negative electric charge, and neutrons have no charge.
- Overall, an atom is neutral.
- The hydrogen atom has no neutrons.
- An element is a type of matter that cannot be split into another substance. An element consists of atoms of the same kind.
- Each element has its own name and symbol, and its own characteristics and uses.
- Each element has a unique position in a chart called the Periodic Table.
- The arrangement of electrons in shells is called the electronic configuration and this can be represented diagrammatically or numerically.

Molecules and compounds

- Elements can be combined physically to form a mixture.
- Elements can be combined chemically to form a compound, which has different properties from the elements. The elements combine in quantities in a fixed proportion.
- In mixtures, the elements can be easily identified and their properties still observed; in compounds they cannot.
- The formation of a mixture is a reversible physical change – the elements can be separated.
- The formation of a compound is a chemical change that is not usually reversible – the elements cannot easily be separated.
- When the compound FeS (iron sulfide) is formed, one atom of Fe combines with one atom of S.
- The combination of elements chemically is called a chemical reaction. It can be represented by a chemical equation:

    $$Fe + S \longrightarrow FeS$$

- The compound formed is a new substance with different properties from the original substances.
- In a molecule, the atoms are bonded together.
- Some elements exist as molecules.
- Some gases, such as oxygen (O_2), exist as molecules that are pairs of atoms bonded together. Such a gas is called a diatomic gas.
- Some elements, such as phosphorus and sulfur, exist as polyatomic molecules.

Review questions on Atoms, molecules and compounds

1. Which of the following is NOT a gas?

    a) Air   **b)** Car exhaust fumes   **c)** Fluffy cotton balls

2. Is an uninflated balloon heavier or lighter than when it is blown up?

    a) Heavier   **b)** Lighter   **c)** The same

3. When a sponge under water is squeezed what escapes?

    a) Soapy water   **b)** Particles of sponge   **c)** Air from the spaces in the sponge

4. Which material is a solid?

    a) Honey   **b)** Oil at room temperature   **c)** Cotton wool

5. To change metal from solid to liquid, you must:

    a) heat it   **b)** cool it   **c)** bend it.

6. Indicate whether the following are true or false.

    a) All liquids keep their volume.

    b) Solids can be cut since their bonds are weak.

    c) A liquid cannot keep a shape.

    d) The bonds in gases keep them from expanding in volume.

    e) A solid will expand to fill its container.

    f) Gases are easy to pour from one container to another.

7. How is matter defined?

8. a) Identify the states in which matter exists.

    b) Give two characteristics of each state.

    c) Illustrate the arrangement of particles in each state.

9. a) Do the particles in a given substance differ?

    b) Name the two factors that determine the state of a substance.

10. Identify the similarity between:

    a) solids and liquids   **b)** liquids and gases.

11. From your experiments, give one factor that is responsible for change of state.

12. Explain what happens to the particles in:

    a) solids as they change to liquids

    b) gases as they change to liquids.

13. Identify two uses of dry ice. For each use, state the property of the dry ice that allows it to have this use.

14. Fig 9.12 shows the changes from solid to liquid to gas and back. What are the numbered processes occuring on each arrow?

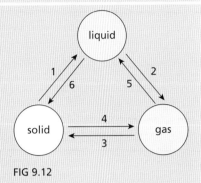

FIG 9.12

15. Define the following terms:

    a) atom

    b) shell

    c) Periodic Table.

16. Which particles does the nucleus contain?

17. The elements of the Periodic Table have been arranged in rows and columns. Explain why they have been arranged in that way.

18. What type of information do the following give about an element?

    a) The period   **b)** The group

19. Complete the information on the charges of the particles below.

    a) Neutrons have _____ charge.

    b) Electrons have _____ charge.

    c) Protons have _____ charge.

20. Copy and complete the following table.

Element	e	n	p	Z	M	Symbol
Nitrogen	7				14	
	10	10				
		2			4	
		16	15			
				4	9	
	5				11	
		10				F

TABLE 9.2

153

21. Draw a simple labelled model of an atom to indicate the position of the protons, neutrons and electrons.

22. Give the position with respect to group (G) and period (P) of the following elements:

a) magnesium   **d)** beryllium   **g)** silicon   **j)** fluorine.
b) lithium   **e)** calcium   **h)** neon
c) sulfur   **f)** oxygen   **i)** aluminium

23. Define the following terms:

a) mixture   **c)** chemical change   **e)** molecule
b) compound   **d)** atom   **f)** polyatomic.

24. Some iron and some sulfur are combined on a sheet of filter paper. Describe one experiment you would carry out to show that the combination is a mixture.

25. Iron and sulfur are combined to form a compound. Give two observations you could make that would indicate the formation of the compound.

26. Oxygen gas is composed of two oxygen atoms. Why is oxygen gas an element?

27. a) Identify the types of effects that heat can have on matter.
    b) Give an example of each type of effect.

28. Why is orange juice categorised as a mixture, and water as a compound?

29. Below are some scientific words from this topic. Find them in the word-search puzzle.

ATOM   CHANGE   CHEMICAL

COMBINATION   COMPOUND   DIATOMIC

ELEMENT   FLAME   GAS

IRON   MIXTURE   MOLECULE

POLYATOMIC   SULFIDE   SULFUR

L	L	F	F	Z	F	W	X	L	N	P	R	Z	I	V
T	M	T	L	E	C	P	I	U	O	F	K	R	R	U
N	A	N	S	A	G	Q	X	C	I	U	O	N	Q	E
D	I	A	T	O	M	I	C	M	T	N	C	H	P	V
C	Q	E	C	U	N	E	O	H	A	I	T	A	X	H
X	O	F	R	L	A	L	T	P	N	C	N	T	P	V
W	Q	M	Z	U	E	U	R	T	I	C	E	O	S	Q
G	K	A	P	C	T	U	K	M	B	H	M	M	C	J
V	E	N	U	O	F	X	O	M	M	E	E	S	C	I
N	L	L	Q	L	U	T	I	U	O	M	L	A	K	L
N	E	N	U	D	A	N	S	M	C	I	E	Q	W	G
M	J	S	U	Y	I	R	D	O	B	C	L	Z	T	G
Q	D	J	L	C	H	A	N	G	E	A	N	T	J	D
Y	N	O	I	V	N	X	X	E	K	L	Q	R	C	E
D	P	P	E	D	I	F	L	U	S	I	E	K	L	J

Unit 10: Forces and energy

We are learning how to:

- understand the action of forces
- represent forces in size and direction
- describe gravitational forces
- relate pressure to the applied forces.

Introduction

In this section, you will find out about forces. You will look at how forces bring about changes and how you can represent forces in drawings. You will also look at different forms of energy and how energy can be transformed from one form into others.

Forces

A force is a push or a pull on one object by another. A force can change the motion and/or shape of an object.

Some forces act only when the objects are in contact. Other forces act when objects are apart.

Forces have both size and direction, so we use arrows to represent forces in diagrams.

Mass and weight

You may think that 'mass' and 'weight' mean the same thing, but you would be wrong. In science, mass is the amount of matter an object contains, while weight is the force with which the object acts downwards due to the pull of gravity.

Pressure is related to force

Pressure is the result of a force acting over an area.

The smaller the surface area, the greater the pressure created by a force.

Energy

In science, energy is the ability to do work.

Work is done when a force acts over a distance. For example, a car does work when it moves up a hill.

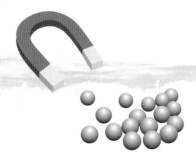

FIG 10.1 Magnetism is a non-contact force

FIG 10.2 A nail has a flat end and a pointed end; pressure is much greater at the pointed end

FIG 10.3 A car doing work

Forms of energy

Although all energy is the same, it has different effects in different contexts. This is easier to understand if we talk about forms of energy. Each form of energy does something different. In this section you will consider lots of different forms of energy, including light, heat, sound, electricity, potential energy and kinetic energy.

FIG 10.4 Energy transformations in a light bulb

When work is done, energy is transformed from one form into others. For example, when you turn a light bulb on, electrical energy is transformed into light energy and heat energy.

Non-renewable and renewable sources of energy

Large-scale sources of energy can be divided into two groups according to how quickly they are replaced by nature.

FIG 10.5 Wind is a renewable source of energy

Some sources, like crude oil, take many millions of years to form, while others, like wind, are continually replenished by natural processes.

> **Challenge**
>
> The Sun is the source of almost all energy on Earth. Can you explain why?

Action of forces

We are learning how to:

- determine the resultant of two or more parallel forces acting on a solid
- understand the action of forces.

Action of forces >>>

Forces can bring about changes to the motion and/or shape of an object.

FIG 10.6 Forces make objects move more quickly or more slowly

A force can make a stationary object move. It can also make a moving object **speed up** or **slow down**. A car travels faster when the driver presses the accelerator, and slower when he or she presses the brake.

FIG 10.7 Forces make objects change direction

A force can make a moving object **change direction**. A car driver uses the steering wheel to change direction.

When cars crash together, the forces involved cause the panels of the car to permanently **change shape**.

FIG 10.8 Forces make objects change shape

Investigating the effects of forces

Here is what you need:

- ping pong ball
- straw.

Here is what you should do:

1. Slowly roll the ball across the table. Using a straw, blow the ball in the direction that it is travelling.

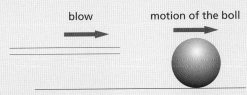

blow   motion of the boll

FIG 10.9

2. What happens to the speed and direction of the ball?

3. Slowly roll the ball across the table. Using a straw, blow the ball in the opposite direction to that in which it is travelling.

4. What happens to the speed and direction of the ball?

5. Slowly roll the ball across the table. Using a straw, blow the ball at right angles to the direction in which it is travelling.

6. What happens to the speed and direction of the ball?

7. Push down on the ball with your thumb.

8. What happens to the shape of the ball?

Check your understanding

1. Fig 10.10 shows different directions in which a rowing boat might move in a river, relative to the flow of the river.

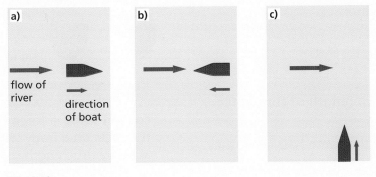

a)   b)   c)

flow of river

direction of boat

FIG 10.10

In each case, state what would happen to the speed and direction of the boat.

Fun fact

Friction is a force that opposes motion and slows things down.

FIG 10.11

Racing cars sometimes need to slow down very quickly. The friction causes the brakes to glow red hot.

Key terms

force a push or a pull

speed up to move more quickly

slow down to move more slowly

change direction to alter the direction of motion

change shape to alter the shape of an object

Types of force

We are learning how to:

- describe the importance of gravitational forces acting on bodies
- identify types of force.

Types of force »»

Forces can be divided into two groups – contact forces and non-contact forces – depending on whether the objects exerting and receiving the force are touching each other.

Contact forces

Contact forces act between objects that are touching, or in contact with, each other.

Friction is a contact force that acts on moving objects that touch each other. Without friction between the bottoms of your shoes and the ground, you would not be able to walk. Your feet would just slide about.

Objects also experience friction when they move through liquids like water, and gases like air. In this case, the friction is called **water resistance** or **air resistance**.

Objects in water or in air experience a force called **buoyancy**. This force acts in the opposite direction to gravity. Buoyancy makes it possible for boats to float on water.

Non-contact forces

Non-contact forces act between objects that are not touching each other. **Gravity** is a non-contact force. Gravity keeps the planets in their orbits. Magnetism is also a non-contact force.

FIG 10.12 Air resistance is a contact force

FIG 10.13 Buoyancy acts in the opposite direction to gravity

FIG 10.14 Magnetism is a non-contact force

FIG 10.15

Activity 10.2

Investigating electrostatic forces

Work with a partner on this activity.
Here is what you need:

- balloons × 2
- sewing thread.

Here is what you should do:

1. Blow the balloons up and tie a length of thread to each one.
2. Rub both of the balloons on the same hair or clothes.
3. Hold the balloons by the cotton threads so the balloons are apart but close together (see Fig 10.15).
4. Are any forces acting between the balloons? If so, are they contact or non-contact forces?

Key terms

contact force a force that acts on a body while actually touching it

non-contact force a force that acts on a body without actually touching it

Activity 10.3

Investigating magnetic forces

Here is what you need:

- bar magnet × 2.

Here is what you should do:

1. Place one magnet on the table and bring the second magnet slowly towards it so that the magnets are end to end.

2. Are any forces acting between the magnets? If so, are they contact or non-contact forces?

3. Turn the magnet on the table through half a turn and bring the second magnet towards it so that the magnets are end to end.

4. Are any forces acting between the magnets? If so, are they contact or non-contact forces?

Check your understanding

1. Six different forces are shown in Fig 10.17.

   Which of these forces is described in each of the following sentences?

   a) A contact force felt as an object moves across a surface.

   b) A non-contact force felt when an object is close to the Earth.

   c) A contact force felt as an object moves through the air.

   d) A non-contact force felt when a magnet is placed near some metal.

   e) A contact force that supports an object floating on water.

   f) A non-contact force felt when an insulator like plastic or rubber has been rubbed.

gravitational force   frictional force

magnetic force   buoyancy

electrostatic force   air resistance

FIG 10.17

Key terms

water resistance the friction experienced by an object moving through water

air resistance the friction experienced by an object moving through air

buoyancy the upward force experienced by an object in a gas or a liquid, which is equal to the weight of gas or liquid it displaces

gravity a force that attracts things towards the centre of the Earth or any other body that has mass

electrostatic the electrical force between electrically charged objects

magnetic the forces between the poles of magnets

Friction

We are learning how to:

• describe the importance of gravitational forces acting on bodies
• explain the force of friction.

Friction 〉〉〉

Whenever one object slides over another, a force works against this movement. This force is called **friction**.

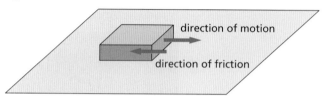

FIG 10.18 Friction is a contact force

The direction of friction is always in the opposite direction to the motion of an object. Friction exists only while an object is in motion.

If you examine the surface of an object that feels perfectly smooth to the touch using a powerful microscope, you will find that it is far from smooth. The surface is really an irregular pattern of high points and low points.

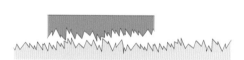

FIG 10.19 Surfaces moving over each other magnified

As an object moves, the high points on the object and the high points on the surface push against each other, so they act to slow the object down.

Activity 10.4

Investigating friction

Here is what you need:

• piece of wood fitted with a hook
• force meter
• weights
• sheet of sandpaper.

Here is what you should do:

1. Place a piece of wood with a hook in it on the table, and attach it to a force meter.

2. Gently pull on the force meter and pull the block at a steady speed.

3. Record the reading on the force meter.

4. Put a weight on top of the block, and pull the block at a steady speed.

5. Record the reading on the force meter.

6. Fix a large sheet of sandpaper to the top of the table so that you can pull the block over it.

7. Pull the block over the sandpaper at a steady speed.

8. Record the reading on the force meter.

9. What two factors affect the size of the friction force? Explain your answer.

Energy is needed to overcome friction. This energy is wasted, in the sense that it is not used to do useful work but is lost as heat. Friction also causes surfaces to wear each other away.

Friction cannot be completely eliminated; however, it can often be reduced by keeping surfaces apart, so that they can pass over each other more easily.

Check your understanding

1. Friction is important in many sports. State whether each of the following increases or decreases friction.

   a) A gymnast rubs chalk on her hands before she grabs the horizontal bars.
   b) A skier waxes the underneath of his skis before skiing down a mountain.
   c) A sprinter wears spiked running shoes.
   d) An ice skater wears skates that have a very thin blade.

Fun fact

On a cold day, rubbing your hands together makes them warm, because the energy needed to overcome the friction between your hands is converted to heat.

Key term

friction a force that opposes the movement of one surface over another

163

Water resistance and air resistance

We are learning how to:

- describe the importance of gravitational forces acting on bodies
- explain water resistance and air resistance.

Water resistance and air resistance

Friction is not restricted to movement between solid surfaces. It also exists when a solid moves through a liquid or gas, and between moving layers of liquids and gases. In this case, we call the forces '**water resistance**' and '**air resistance**'.

The amount of friction experienced as an object passes through a liquid or gas depends very much on its shape.

Most fish are long and flat. They experience very little resistance, so they can move quickly through the water.

Parachutes are spread out. They experience a large amount of resistance, so the parachutist can descend to the ground slowly.

Resistance makes it more difficult for an object to move through water or air. Energy is wasted as heat.

Modern cars, aircraft and boats have shapes that reduce resistance to a minimum. This is called **streamlining**. Moving a streamlined shape uses less fuel and makes the vehicle more efficient.

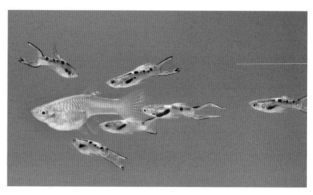

FIG 10.20 Fish move quickly through water

FIG 10.21 Parachutists move more slowly through the air

Activity 10.5

Investigating resistance and shape

Here is what you need:

- modelling clay
- tall clear container, such as a large measuring cylinder
- cooking oil
- rod – long enough to reach the bottom of the container
- stopwatch.

FIG 10.22 Modern cars are streamlined

Here is what you should do:

1. Take a piece of modelling clay. Roll it into a ball and then divide it into four pieces of approximately equal mass.

2. Make four different shapes (a–d) out of the four pieces.

3. Pour cooking oil into a tall clear container, until the level is about 2 cm from the top.

4. Hold one of the shapes so that it is just touching the surface of the cooking oil. Release the shape and start timing.

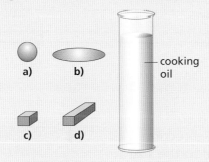

FIG 10.23

5. Stop timing when the clay piece touches the bottom of the measuring cylinder.

6. Remove the clay piece from the oil by pushing a long rod into the shape and lifting it out.

7. Repeat Steps 4–6 for each shape.

8. Record your results in a table.

9. Draw a bar chart to illustrate your results

Check your understanding

1.

FIG 10.25

Say how the labelled features in Fig 10.25 help the cyclist to go faster.

Key terms

water resistance the friction experienced by an object moving through water

air resistance the friction experienced by an object moving through air

streamlined shaped in such a way as to minimise the effects of water resistance or air resistance

Representing forces

We are learning how to:

- investigate the relationship between an applied force and pressure
- represent forces.

Representing forces

Forces have both size, or **magnitude**, and **direction**. Magnitude means size: forces can be large in size or small in size. We measure the size of a force in units called **newtons**. We can represent forces in a diagram using arrows.

5 N   3 N   1 N

FIG 10.26 Forces of different magnitude acting in the same direction

The forces represented by the arrows in Fig 10.26 are different magnitudes but are acting in the same direction. Notice that the length of the line is proportional to the size of the force. The line representing a force of 5 newtons (5 N) is five times longer than the line representing a force of 1 N.

3 N   3 N   3 N   3 N

FIG 10.27 Forces of the same magnitude acting in different directions

The forces represented by the arrows in Fig 10.27 are **equal** in magnitude but they are acting in different directions.

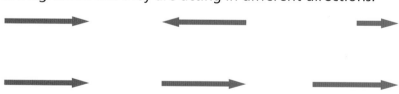

FIG 10.28 Forces that are equal and forces that are not equal

For two forces to be equal, they must be both equal in magnitude and acting in the same direction.

Measuring forces

Here is what you need:

- force meter (0–10 N)
- small objects with loops of string attached
- ruler.

Here is what you should do:

1. Place an object on the table in front of you.

2. Attach a force meter to the object and pull the object in a straight line.

FIG 10.29

3. Read the value on the force meter as you pull the object.

4. Using a scale in which 1 centimetre (1 cm) represents 1 N, draw the force. Remember that you must represent both the magnitude of the force and its direction.

5. Repeat Steps 1–4 on some different forces. Pull each force in a different direction.

Fun fact

Quantities that have only magnitude are called scalars. Quantities that have both magnitude and direction are called vectors. Forces are vectors.

Check your understanding

1. The arrows in Fig 10.30 represent six forces, A–F.

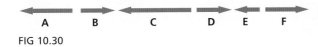

FIG 10.30

a) Which arrow represents the largest force?

b) Which arrow represents the smallest force?

c) Which arrows represent a pair of forces equal in magnitude but opposite in direction?

d) Which arrows represent a pair of equal forces?

Key terms

force a push or a pull

magnitude the size of something

direction The path that something moves along

newton the SI unit of force, 1 N = 1 kg m/s^2

equal to have the same value or amount

Resultant of forces acting along the same line

We are learning how to:

- investigate the relationship between an applied force and pressure
- investigate resultants of forces acting along a straight line.

Resultant of forces acting along the same line »»

Forces acting along the same line either act in the same direction or in opposite directions.

FIG 10.31 Forces acting along the same line

We can add two forces acting along the same line. To do this, we replace the two forces by a single force, called the **resultant**. The resultant has the equivalent effect of the two forces.

3 N   3 N   6 N

forces   resultant

FIG 10.32 Resultant of two forces acting in a line

A single force of 6 N acting from left to right has the same effect as two forces of 3 N acting from left to right.

3 N   3 N   6 N

+   =

forces   resultant

FIG 10.33 Forces acting in the same direction

In effect, we are adding the two 3 N forces together to get their resultant.

We find the resultant of forces acting in the opposite direction along the same line in the same way.

3 N   2 N   1 N

+   =

forces   resultant

FIG 10.34 Forces acting in opposite directions

We can think of forces acting in opposite directions as being positive and negative. In this case, the 2 N force acts from right to left so the resultant will be 3 N – 2 N = 1 N.

Activity 10.7

Drawing resultants

Here is what you need:

- ruler.

Here is what you should do:

1. Fig 10.35 shows four forces that act along the same line.

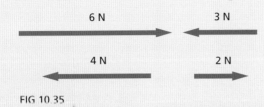

FIG 10.35

2. Using your ruler, draw the resultant of each pair of forces. Remember that the length of the line representing a force is proportional to its magnitude.

You can use the same method to find the resultant of three or more forces acting along the same line.

FIG 10.36 Adding forces in the same direction

The resultant of forces of 4 N and 3 N acting in the same direction is a single force of 7 N in that direction.

FIG 10.37 Adding forces in opposite directions

The resultant of forces of 7 N and 2 N acting in opposite directions is a single force of 5 N acting in the same direction as the force of 7 N.

FIG 10.38 Resultant of three forces acting along the same line

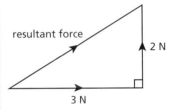
Key terms

force a push or a pull

resultant a single force that has the same total effect as two or more other forces

Check your understanding

1. Fig 10.40 shows a tug of war.

   a) Predict which team will win.

   b) Explain why you think this team will win, giving the value of the resultant force

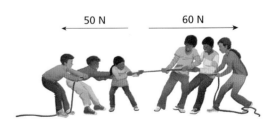

FIG 10.40

Mass and weight

We are learning how to:

- discuss the importance of gravitational forces acting on bodies
- explain the difference between mass and weight.

Mass and weight ⟩⟩

Mass

In simple terms, the **mass** of an object is the quantity of matter that it contains. A better definition of mass can be obtained by considering **inertia**.

Inertia is the reluctance of a stationary body to move. The larger the mass of a stationary body, the more difficult it is to move. Also, when the body is in motion, the more difficult it is to stop.

We can say, therefore, that the mass of a body is a measure of its inertia.

FIG 10.41 A large lorry has a large mass and a lot of inertia

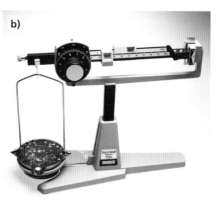

FIG 10.42 Laboratory balances: **a)** electronic balance and **b)** beam balance

Mass is measured on a balance. Two types of balance are in common use in laboratories: the beam balance and the electronic balance.

The mass of an object is the same no matter where the mass is measured. The units of mass are the kilogram (kg), for large masses, and the gram (g), for small masses. For even smaller masses, the milligram (mg) may also be used.

$$1 \text{ kg} = 1000 \text{ g} \qquad 1 \text{ g} = 1000 \text{ mg}$$

Weight

In everyday English, the terms 'mass' and '**weight**' are often used in a way that suggests they mean the same thing, but

FIG 10.43 Force meter

this is not the case in science. Weight is a force exerted by an object towards the ground due to the pull of **gravity**. Like all forces, weight is measured in newtons (N).

The weight of an object is measured using a force meter. This looks like a spring balance but is calibrated in newtons not grams.

Activity 10.8

Investigating the relationship between mass and weight

Here is what you need:

- force meter
- masses of 0.2–1.0 kg
- graph paper.

Here is what you should do:

1. Construct a table of masses and weights of 0–1 kg in 0.2 kg increments to record your measurements.

2. Hang a 0.2 kg mass on the force meter and measure its weight. Record the value.

3. Add another 0.2 kg mass on the force meter and measure its weight. Record the value.

4. Repeat Step 3 until you have a complete set of measurements up to 1 kg.

5. Plot a graph of weight on the vertical axis, or y-axis, against mass on the horizontal axis, or x-axis. Draw the line of best fit through the points.

6. Calculate the gradient of your graph.

The weight of an object depends on the pull of gravity. On the Earth, the weight of a mass of 1 kg is about 10 N.

On Earth, the pull of gravity is more or less constant, so the weight of an object does not change, However, if an object was taken to the Moon or to another planet where the pull of gravity is different to that on Earth, the weight of the object would change.

Fun fact

The pull of gravity on the Moon is only about one-sixth that on the Earth. An object will therefore weigh less on the Moon than it does on the Earth.

FIG 10.44 A lunar landing craft

The mass of a lunar landing craft is about 15 000 kg. On the Earth, the weight of the landing craft is 150 000 N. On the Moon, however, the weight of the landing craft is about 25 000 N.

Key terms

mass the amount of matter an object contains

inertia the reluctance of an object to move or to change its motion

weight the downward force acting when an object is attracted by gravity

gravity a force that attracts things towards the centre of the Earth or any other body that has mass

Check your understanding

1. What is the difference between a person's mass and weight?

2. The mass of a person is 55 kg. What is their weight?

171

Gravity

We are learning how to:

• discuss the importance of gravitational forces acting on bodies
• calculate the weight of an object in different places.

Gravity >>>

Gravity is the force that holds objects on the Earth and pulls objects towards the ground. If we drop an object from the air, it will fall to the ground with an acceleration of 9.8 m/s^2. This value is the acceleration due to gravity.

The **weight** of an object depends on both its mass and on the acceleration due to gravity. The following equation shows how mass, weight and acceleration due to gravity (g) are related:

$$\text{weight (N)} = \text{mass (kg)} \times g \text{ (m/s}^2)$$

Since the value of g on Earth is 9.8 m/s^2, we can rewrite the equation as:

$$\text{weight (N)} = \text{mass (kg)} \times 9.8 \text{ (m/s}^2)$$

The value of g is often taken to be 10 m/s^2 in order to make approximate calculations.

FIG 10.45 Objects always fall towards the ground

Activity 10.9

Finding your mass and weight

Here is what you need:

• bathroom scales.

Here is what you should do:

1. If necessary, set the display on the bathroom scales to display kilograms.
2. Take off your shoes and stand on the scales.
3. Record your mass in kilograms.
4. Find your weight in newtons by multiplying your mass by 9.8.

Everything that has mass also has gravity. All objects are therefore attracted towards each other.

When the masses of objects are small, such as the masses of people, the **forces of attraction** are very weak. However, when the masses are large, such as the masses of planets, the forces of attraction are very strong.

Fun fact

FIG 10.46 A space ship in orbit around the Earth

Astronauts inside an orbiting spacecraft experience a feeling of weightlessness or 'zero g', because the orbit the spacecraft follows around the Earth means both the spacecraft and the astronauts are 'free-falling' constantly towards the Earth. This means that the astronauts do not constantly experience other types of force that cause the sensation of weight, such as mechanical pushes from the floor and other surfaces.

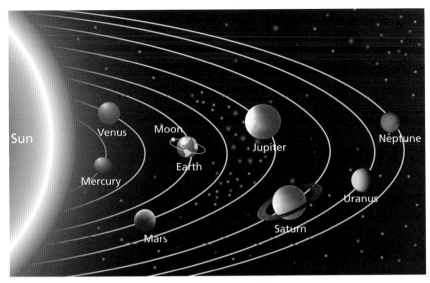

FIG 10.47 The Solar System

The planets continuously move in orbit around the Sun. Only the forces of attraction between the Sun and the planets keep the planets in orbit and prevent them flying off into space.

Similarly, the Moon is held in orbit around the Earth by the gravitational forces of attraction between the Moon and the Earth.

An object is sometimes described as becoming '**weightless**' in outer space. This does not mean that the object ceases to have any mass. The mass of an object does not change from place to place and will always be the same number of kilograms.

An object may be described as 'weightless' in outer space, beyond the effect of the Sun and planets, because the acceleration due to gravity is zero. If an object was taken out into space beyond the gravitational pull of any of the bodies in the Solar System, then g would equal 0 and therefore:

$$\text{weight} = \text{mass} \times 0 = 0$$

Any object in outer space is therefore weightless.

Check your understanding

1. An astronaut in a space suit has a mass of 120 kg.

   a) What is the astronaut's weight on the Earth? (On the Earth, $g = 9.8 \text{ m/s}^2$.)

   b) What is the astronaut's mass on the Moon?

   c) What is the astronaut's weight on the Moon? (On the Moon, $g = 1.6 \text{ m/s}^2$.)

   d) What would be her weight in outer space? (In outer space, $g = 0 \text{ m/s}^2$.)

Key terms

gravity a force that attracts things towards the centre of the Earth or any other body that has mass

weight the downward force acting when an object is attracted by gravity

force of attraction a force that pulls objects towards each other

weightless a condition that exists when an object is sufficiently far away from any object in space that it experiences no gravitational forces of attraction, and therefore has no weight

Weight in places other than on Earth

Weight in places other than on Earth 》》

Since weight depends on the value of g (the **acceleration due to gravity**), the weight of an object will change if the object is taken somewhere other than the Earth where the value of g is different.

The acceleration due to gravity is different on each of the **planets** of the Solar System. An object has the same mass but a different weight on each planet. Table 10.1 gives the value for the acceleration due to gravity at the surface of all the planets in the Solar System.

Planet	Acceleration due to gravity in m/s²
Mercury	3.6
Venus	8.9
Earth	9.8
Mars	3.8
Jupiter	26.0
Saturn	11.1
Uranus	10.7
Neptune	14.1
Moon	1.6

TABLE 10.1 Acceleration due to gravity on the planets in the Solar System (note that although the Moon is listed here, it is not a planet, but a satellite of Earth)

The acceleration due to gravity at the surface of a planet is greatest on the giant planet Jupiter (Fig 10.49). An object will weigh more on Jupiter than on any of the other planets.

Conversely, the acceleration due to gravity is least on Mercury (Fig 10.48). An object will weigh least on the planet Mercury.

FIG 10.48 Mercury, the smallest planet, has the smallest acceleration due to gravity

FIG 10.49 Jupiter, the largest planet, has the largest acceleration due to gravity

Activity 10.10

Here is what you need:

- Table 10.1.

Here is what you should do:

1. Calculate your weight at the surface of each planet in the Solar System. Write your answers in a table.

2. On which planet would your weight be nearest to its value on Earth?

Check your understanding

1. Fig 10.50 shows the Mars rover 'Opportunity'. It has been placed on the surface of Mars to gather information about the planet.

FIG 10.50

The mass of the rover is 185 kg. Use the values in Table 10.1 to answer the following:

    a) What is the weight of the rover on Earth?
    b) What is the mass of the rover on Mars?
    c) What is the weight of the rover on Mars?

Key terms

acceleration due to gravity the acceleration of an object towards the earth due to the pull of gravity

planet a large round body, made up either of rocks or gases, orbiting a star

Force and pressure

We are learning how to:

- investigate the relationship between an applied force and pressure
- explain the link between force and pressure.

Force and pressure »»

Every object exerts a **force** downwards due to the pull of gravity. This force is called its **weight**.

Although the weight of an object is constant, the object may not always exert the same **pressure**. The pressure exerted by an object on the ground depends both on its weight and on the **area** of contact with the ground.

FIG 10.52 Which shoes are best suited to walking on soft sand?

Sand is soft and often difficult to walk over. Sand shoes have a large area, so the weight of the person wearing them is spread out. This means that the person only exerts a small pressure on the sand.

If the same person attempted to walk on sand in stiletto heels, they would sink. Stiletto heels have only a small surface area. The weight is concentrated in a small area, so the person would exert a large pressure on the sand.

Activity 10.11

Investigating the effects of pressure

Here is what you need:

- large tray of dry sand
- house brick that has faces of three different sizes.

Here is what you should do:

1. Smooth the surface of the sand.

2. Carefully place the brick on the sand so that the face of the brick with the largest surface area is in contact with the sand. Gently remove the brick and examine the imprint.

3. Repeat this twice using faces of the brick with different surface areas.

4. Compare the imprints left by all three faces of the brick.

5. Which face left the deepest imprint and which left the shallowest imprint?

6. Explain your observations.

The following equation connects force, pressure and area:

$$\text{pressure} = \frac{\text{force}}{\text{area}}$$

When force is expressed in newtons, and area in metres squared, the unit of pressure is the newton per square meter (N/m^2), which is also called the pascal (Pa).

For example, if a force of 4000 N acts on an area of 1.6 m^2 then the pressure exerted = 4000 ÷ 1.6 = 2500 Pa, or 2.5 kPa.

Pressure is sometimes expressed in newtons per centimetre squared (N/cm^2) when the surface in contact is small and it is more appropriate to measure the dimensions in centimetres.

Check your understanding

1. Fig 10.54 represents a concrete block of dimensions 3 m × 2 m × 1 m. The weight of the block is 150 000 N.

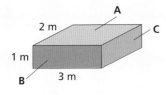

FIG 10.54

a) Calculate the pressure exerted by the block on the ground if it is stood on side A, on side B and on side C.

b) The weight of the block is constant. Explain why, if the block is placed on boggy ground, it will sink in more if placed on side C than on side A.

Key terms

force a push or a pull

weight the downward force acting when an object is attracted by gravity

pressure the force per unit area applied perpendicularly to a surface

area the amount of a surface

Pressure and gases

We are learning how to:

- investigate the relationship between an applied force and pressure
- explain how gases exert pressure.

Pressure and gases ≫

The particles in a gas move about very quickly, and there are relatively large distances between them.

When a gas is placed in a sealed container, the particles collide with each other and also with the walls of the container. The collisions of the particles with the walls of the container create **pressure**.

When a gas particle collides with the walls of its container, it exerts a **force** on it. The more particles that collide with the walls, the greater that force. The pressure the particles create on the walls of a container is equal to the total force acting on the walls divided by the area over which the particles are colliding.

Changes in gas pressure can be detected using an instrument called a **manometer**. A manometer consists of a U tube that contains coloured water or mercury. (The water is coloured with ink or dye to make it easier to see the level.)

A manometer compares the pressure on either side of the U tube. When the manometer is not connected to a container, atmospheric pressure acts equally on both sides, and the level of liquid in both sides is the same.

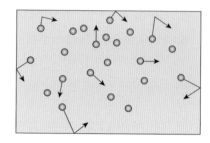

FIG 10.55 Particles continually collide with the walls of their container

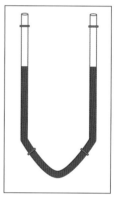

FIG 10.56 A simple manometer

Activity 10.12

Investigating changes in pressure using a manometer

Here is what you need:

- clear plastic tubing
- water coloured with red ink
- small filter funnel
- board with clamps or stand and clamp, × 2
- ruler.

Here is what you should do:

1. Make a U tube out of clear plastic tubing.

2. Clamp your U tube to a board or suspend it between two stands and clamps.

3. Using a small funnel, pour coloured water into the tube until the water is about halfway up each side of the U tube.

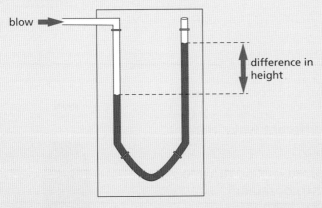

blow

difference in height

FIG 10.57

4. Gently blow down one side of the U tube. Place your finger over the end of the tube you have just blown down.

5. Measure the difference in height between the liquid in each of the sides of the U tube.

6. Remove your finger and observe what happens to the level of liquid in each side of the manometer.

7. Gently suck one side of the U tube. (If you suck too hard you will end up with a mouthful of coloured water.) Place your finger over the end of the tube you have just sucked.

8. Measure the difference in height between the liquid in each of the legs of the U tube.

9. What happens to the heights of the liquid in each side of the U tube when the pressure exerted on each side is not the same?

If the pressure on each side of the U tube is not the same, the height of the liquid in each side will no longer be equal. Additional pressure forces the level of liquid down on one side and up on the other. The greater the pressure difference, the greater the difference in height of the liquid in the two legs.

Check your understanding

1. Explain in terms of the action of the particles why the pressure in the barrel of a bicycle pump increases when you put your finger over the hole at the end and push the piston down.

Fun fact

The average speed of the particles depends on the temperature of the gas. At room temperature, the speed of the particles is of the order of 500 m/s. Each particle collides with other particles many times per second.

Key terms

pressure the force per unit area applied perpendicularly to a surface

force a push or a pull

manometer a device for comparing the pressure of gases

179

Everyday examples of pressure

We are learning how to:

- investigate the relationship between an applied force and pressure
- explain everyday examples of pressure.

Everyday examples of pressure ⟩⟩

Pressure comes into our lives in lots of different ways. Here are some examples.

Carbonated or fizzy drinks contain dissolved carbon dioxide gas. The pressure of carbon dioxide in the container is slightly more than atmospheric pressure. When the container is opened, some of the carbon dioxide comes out of solution as bubbles in the drink.

Bicycle and car tyres contain air under high pressure. The actual pressure may be anything from 25 to 60 times atmospheric pressure. This allows the tyre to distort when going over a bump, so that the passenger has a comfortable ride.

Water is supplied to our homes under pressure. When we open a tap, the water flows out. We can increase the pressure of water flowing out of a garden hose by covering part of the end. This makes the water squirt further.

Blood is pumped through the blood vessels in the body by pressure created by the heart. Doctors sometimes measure a person's blood pressure as a way of checking whether the person's heart is working properly.

FIG 10.58 Fizzy drinks contain dissolved carbon dioxide gas; the gas at the top of this bottle is under pressure

FIG 10.59 Bicycle and car tyres contain air under high pressure

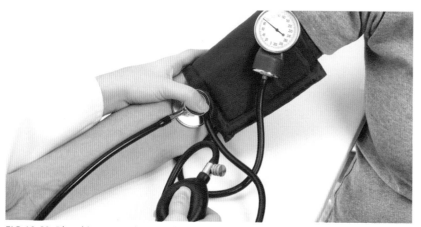

FIG 10.60 Blood is pumped around the body by pressure; this sphygmomanometer measures blood pressure

FIG 10.61 Water comes out of a garden hose under pressure

We can force a tack into a wall by pushing on it with our thumb. The surface area of the point is much smaller than the flat end, so the **force** exerted by the thumb creates a large pressure at the point.

FIG 10.62 A thumb tack

FIG 10.63 Some water birds have big feet

Some water birds, like the purple gallinule, have big feet. This spreads their weight over a large area. The pressure exerted by their feet is small enough to allow them to walk on the floating leaves of aquatic plants.

Check your understanding

1. Fig 10.65 shows a garden sprinkler. It has a row of tiny holes.

FIG 10.65

Explain in terms of pressure why a garden sprinkler is able to make the water spread further than if the water was just allowed to pour out of the end of the hose.

Key terms

pressure the force per unit area applied perpendicularly to a surface

force a push or a pull

Unit 11: Energy transformations

We are learning how to:

- understand what energy is
- tell different forms of energy apart.

What is energy? »»

Energy is the ability to do work.

Although all energy is the same, it has different effects in different contexts. Different forms of energy do different things.

For example, a television produces **light** energy, which we can see, and **sound** energy, which we can hear. It also produces some **heat** energy that we can feel if we touch the back of the device after it has been switched on for a short time. Light, sound and heat are all energy, but they are different because the energy does different things.

FIG 11.1 A television produces light energy, sound energy and heat energy

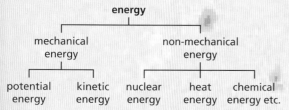

FIG 11.2 Forms of energy

Our bodies have senses that allow us to detect some forms of energy. Our eyes detect light energy, our ears detect sound energy, and our skin detects heat energy.

We are only aware of other forms of energy because we can sense the effects they have. For example, we cannot see **electrical energy** in a wire, but we can sense the effect of electricity in a circuit. When an electric current passes through a bulb it lights up, which we can see, and it gives out heat, which we can feel.

Forms of energy include: heat energy, light energy, sound energy, electrical energy, **chemical energy**, **nuclear energy**, **potential energy** and **kinetic** (movement) **energy**.

Fun fact

The Sun produces twice as much energy in one hour as the entire population of the Earth uses in one year.

FIG 11.3 The Sun

Only a small fraction of the energy produced by the Sun reaches the Earth.

Energy can be classified as mechanical or non-mechanical (see Fig 11.2).

Mechanical energy includes kinetic energy (movement energy) and potential energy (stored energy).

Non-mechanical energy includes light, heat, sound, electrical energy and nuclear energy.

Activity 11.1

Investigating devices associated with different forms of energy

Here is what you need:

- the photographs in Fig 11.4
- your teacher may also provide some devices or pictures for you to examine.

 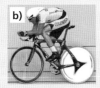 

FIG 11.4

Here is what you should do:

1. For each device, write the name of one form of energy that you associate with it.

2. Write your results in a table. On one side write the name of the device, and on the other write the name of the form of energy.

Check your understanding

1. What forms of energy are associated with the three pictures in Fig 11.5?

FIG 11.5 Different forms of energy

Key terms

light a form of energy that we can see with our eyes

sound a form of energy that we can hear with our ears

heat a form of energy that is transferred as a result of difference in temperature

electrical energy a form of energy easily conducted by metals and easily converted to heat, light and other forms

chemical energy a form of energy in food and fuel

nuclear energy a form of energy obtained from nuclear reactions

potential energy a form of energy stored in an object by virtue of its position, composition or shape

kinetic energy the energy an object has because it is moving

Potential energy

We are learning how to:

- investigate the different types of potential energy.

Potential energy >>>

Potential energy is one form of mechanical energy: it is energy that is stored in some way in a system. Potential energy may be classified as gravitational, chemical or elastic potential energy.

If an object is held in the air and released, it will fall to the ground without anyone exerting a force on it (see Fig 11.6). It is pulled towards the ground by the force of gravity. Any object above the ground is said to have **gravitational potential energy**.

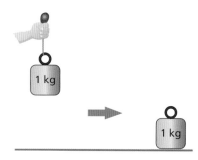

FIG 11.6 Gravitational potential energy

Food contains chemicals that are broken down in the digestive system. The products of digestion provide energy for the many processes in the body. Similarly, fuels contain chemicals that release energy when they are burned. Both food and fuels are examples of **chemical potential energy** (see Fig 11.7).

FIG 11.7 Chemical potential energy in: **a)** food **b)** fuel

If we place a weight on a spring, the spring gets longer (see Fig 11.8). The extended spring has **elastic potential energy**. If we remove the weight, the spring will return to its original shape.

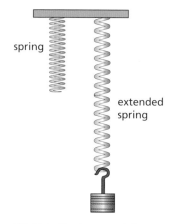

FIG 11.8 Elastic potential energy

Investigating elastic potential energy

Here is what you need:

- elastic band
- clothes peg
- matchstick
- measuring tape.

Here is what you should do:

1. Look at Fig 11.9. Stretch the elastic band over the length of the clothes peg.

2. Open the clothes peg and, making sure that the clothes peg is not pointing at anyone, push the matchstick into it. This pushes part of the elastic band back.

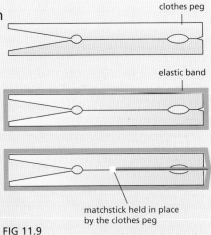

clothes peg

elastic band

matchstick held in place by the clothes peg

FIG 11.9

3. Close the clothes peg.

4. Make sure the clothes peg is not pointing at anyone. Open the clothes peg.

5. Measure how far the matchstick travels.

6. Repeat Steps 1–5 with some different elastic bands.

7. How will you be able to tell which elastic band stores the most potential energy?

1. Fig 11.11 shows a boulder on the edge of a cliff.

   a) What type of energy does the boulder have?

   b) Explain your answer.

FIG 11.11 Balanced Rock, Colorado, US

Fun fact

Electrical energy can be considered a form of potential energy. An electric current flows as a result of a difference in energy levels. The two ends of a battery have different potential energies. An electric current flows from one to the other.

FIG 11.10 An electric current flows between points with different energies

Key terms

gravitational potential energy the energy an object has by virtue of its position above the ground

chemical potential energy the energy stored in a substance due to the chemicals it contains

elastic potential energy the energy stored when an elastic object, such as a spring, is deformed (stretched or compressed)

Kinetic energy

We are learning how to:

- describe how kinetic energy arises
- investigate how gravitational potential energy is converted to kinetic energy and back again.

Kinetic energy ⟫

Kinetic energy is the energy associated with movement. Any moving object has kinetic energy.

Objects that move slowly, like snails, have only a small amount of kinetic energy.

FIG 11.12 **a)** Snail – small amount of kinetic energy. **b)** Dragster – large amount of kinetic energy

Objects that move quickly, like dragsters, have a large amount of kinetic energy.

A **pendulum** consists of a small weight attached to a string. The string is fixed at the opposite end to the weight, so the weight can swing to and fro.

When a pendulum swings, the energy of the pendulum bob continually changes between **gravitational potential energy** and kinetic energy.

FIG 11.13 A pendulum

Activity 11.3

Converting between potential energy and kinetic energy

Here is what you need:

- small weight
- string
- stand and clamp.

Here is what you should do:

1. Make a pendulum by tying a small weight to a length of string. Hang your pendulum on a stand and clamp, or in some other suitable place.

2. Hold the pendulum to one side so it is stationary (point A in Fig 11.14) and then release it.

3. Watch the motion of the pendulum as it swings to and fro through points A, B and C.

4. Copy and complete Table 11.1 with position A, B or C. Assume that the pendulum does not lose any energy as it swings.

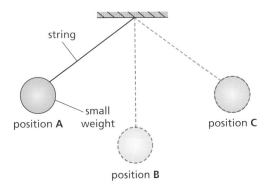

FIG 11.14

	Gravitational potential energy	Kinetic energy
Maximum		
Minimum		

TABLE 11.1

5. How do you know that the pendulum *does* lose energy as it swings?

At the start of the swing, the bob is stationary, so it has no kinetic energy. It is also at the maximum height above the ground or the table, so its gravitational potential energy is at a maximum.

When the bob is midway through its swing, the gravitational potential energy is at a minimum value. The lost potential energy has been converted to kinetic energy. The kinetic energy is at its maximum value.

As the bob continues through its swing, the gravitational potential energy starts to increase. This energy must come from somewhere: kinetic energy is being converted back to potential energy.

Check your understanding

1. Draw diagrams to show the position of a pendulum bob when:

   a) its kinetic energy is greatest

   b) its gravitational potential energy is greatest.

Fun fact

If there was no loss of energy, a pendulum bob would continue to swing forever. In reality, a small amount of energy is lost during each swing, because of friction with the air and friction where the string is suspended. The height to which the bob swings slowly decreases until eventually the pendulum stops.

Key terms

kinetic energy the energy an object has because it is moving

pendulum a weight hung on a rod or string so that it can swing freely

gravitational potential energy the energy an object has by virtue of its position above the ground

Heat and light energy

We are learning how to:

- investigate heat and light energy
- investigate how light travels in straight lines.

Heat and light energy ≫

Heat and **light** are two forms of **energy** that we often experience together.

FIG 11.15 The Sun provides heat and light

The Sun is a major source of heat and light. Daytime is light and warm. Nighttime is dark and cooler.

A light bulb contains a thin wire called a filament. When electricity passes through the filament, the wire gets so hot that it gives out light.

FIG 11.16 A light bulb provides heat and light

FIG 11.17 Burning fuels produce heat and light

When we burn fuels like wood, both heat and light energy are produced.

Activity 11.4

Transforming light energy into electrical energy and back into light energy

Here is what you will need:

- solar cell
- lamp
- wires.

Here is what you should do:

solar cell

1. In an area of good light, for example near a window, make the circuit shown in Fig 11.18. A solar cell transforms light energy into electricity.

2. How does a lamp provide evidence that electricity flows around the circuit?

3. Cover the solar cell so it doesn't receive any light. Does the lamp light up?

lamp

FIG 11.18

4. Carry your circuit to different places in the laboratory where the light intensity varies from very dim to very bright and note the brightness of the lamp.

5. Comment on the link between the brightness of the light and the amount of electricity produced by the solar cell.

6. What can you conclude about the way in which light travels? For example, can light travel around corners?

Light and heat travel from place to place as waves. In Activity 11.4, you discovered that light only travels in straight lines. This is sometimes referred to as 'rectilinear propagation'.

Check your understanding

1. Copy and complete the following sentences:

    a) Heat and light are forms of ....
    b) Heat and light are both given out when a .... burns.
    c) Heat and light travel as ....
    d) Light can only travel in ....
       ....

Key terms

heat a form of energy that is transferred as a result of a difference in temperature

light a form of energy that we can see with our eyes

energy the ability to do work

189

Sound energy

We are learning how to:

• investigate sound energy and how it can be detected.

Sound energy ⟩⟩⟩

Sound is a form of **energy** that we can detect with our ears. **Sound** is produced when an object vibrates. It passes through a medium as sound waves.

We are most used to hearing sounds that travel through air, but sound can also travel through liquids and even solids. If you put your ear to one end of your table and ask a classmate to scratch the other end, you will be able to hear the sound travelling through the table.

FIG 11.20 Sound travels through air

FIG 11.21 Sound travels through solids

Table 11.2 shows the speed of sound in different media. Sound travels fastest in solids and slowest in gases.

Medium	Example	Speed of sound in m/s
gas	air	340
liquid	seawater	1500
solid	steel	5000

TABLE 11.2

The space between the Earth and the Sun is a vacuum. It does not contain any solids, liquids or gases. Many massive violent explosions take place on the surface of the Sun each year. We cannot hear these explosions on Earth because sound cannot travel through the vacuum of space.

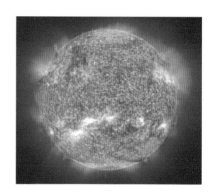

FIG 11.22 Sound cannot travel across a vacuum; the nuclear reactions taking place in the Sun are very loud, but we cannot hear them

Activity 11.5

Making a string telephone

Here is what you need:

- empty can with the top removed × 2
- length of string
- hammer
- small nail.

Here is what you should do:

1. Place an empty can on your desk, open end downwards.

2. Use a small nail and a hammer to make a small hole in the end of the can. The hole needs to be just large enough for the string to pass through.

3. Repeat Step 2 with a second can.

4. Thread string through the hole in the first can and tie several knots in it so that the string cannot be pulled out.

5. Thread the other end of the string through the second can and tie knots to keep it in place.

6. With a partner, move the cans apart until the string is taut. One person should put the can to their mouth and say something while the other person puts the can to their ear to listen.

7. How do the sound waves travel from one can to the other?

Check your understanding

1. How does an object produce sound?

2. Through which type of material (solid, liquid or gas) does sound travel:

   a) fastest?

   b) slowest?

3. Why can people on Earth not hear loud explosions that occur on the Sun?

Fun fact

Sound waves can be used to locate objects under water.

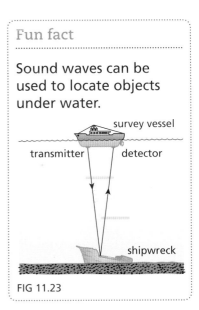

FIG 11.23

Key terms

energy the ability to do work

sound a form of energy that we can hear with our ears

Electrical energy

We are learning how to:

- generate, supply and use electrical energy.

Electrical energy >>>

Electrical energy, or **electricity**, is a very convenient and useful form of energy.

Electricity is generated from other forms of energy in power stations. It is sent to homes and factories along cables, which are either suspended on poles or buried underground.

FIG 11.24 Electricity power lines

Electricity is supplied to homes and businesses through electricity meters that record how much electrical energy has been used. Consumers must pay for the electrical energy they use at the end of each month.

FIG 11.25 An electricity meter

Inside the home, electricity is supplied to each room by wires. Lights are turned on and off by switches, while electrical appliances are made to work by plugging them into sockets.

FIG 11.26 Electricity sockets

Most homes have a range of electrical appliances that change electrical energy into other forms of energy. You will learn more about these later in this section.

Activity 11.6

Survey of electrical appliances

Here is what you should do:

1. Make a list of electrical appliances that people have in their homes.

2. Place these devices into different groups according to what sort of energy an appliance produces.

   Some devices might fit into more than one group. For example, a hairdryer produces heat but it also has a fan that produces kinetic energy.

Check your understanding

1. Where is electricity generated?

2. How is electricity sent from where it is generated to where it is needed?

3. How does the electricity company know how much electrical energy each consumer has used?

4. How is electricity supplied to an electrical appliance?

Key terms

electrical energy another term for electricity

electricity a form of energy that can be transferred from place to place along metal wires as an electric current

Nuclear energy

We are learning how to:

- produce nuclear energy using nuclear fusion or fission
- use the principle of conservation of mass and energy.

Nuclear energy >>>

In order to account for the heat and light provided by the Sun, early scientists suggested the Sun might be a huge ball of burning coal. Such ideas were soon rejected for various reasons. Not until the discovery of **nuclear energy** were scientists able to explain the source of energy of the Sun.

The Sun's source of energy is a process called **nuclear fusion**. Under the conditions of high temperatures and a huge gravitational field, small atoms combine to form larger atoms.

FIG 11.28 The Sun produces massive amounts of energy

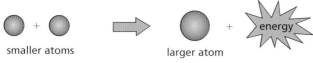

smaller atoms   larger atom   energy

FIG 11.29 Nuclear fusion

The mass of the larger atom is slightly less than the mass of the two smaller atoms that formed it. The missing mass has been converted to energy.

FIG 11.30 A nuclear power station transforms nuclear energy into electricity

A different type of nuclear reaction called **nuclear fission** takes place in a nuclear power station. In this reaction, large atoms of a nuclear fuel like uranium break down to become smaller atoms.

larger atom   smaller atoms

FIG 11.31 Nuclear fission

The mass of the smaller atoms produced is slightly less than the mass of the large atom from which they were formed. The missing mass has been converted to energy.

Nuclear energy results from changes to the nuclei of atoms. During both nuclear fusion and nuclear fission atoms of some elements are destroyed and atoms of other elements are created.

Nuclear energy is different from energy obtained from chemical reactions like burning. In chemical reactions, atoms are rearranged to make new substances but they are not destroyed or created.

Conservation of mass and energy

The principle of conservation of energy states that **energy cannot be created or destroyed**. Since nuclear reactions involve the loss of mass and the creation of energy, we need a new principle that takes nuclear reactions into account.

The principle must be modified to take into account both mass and energy. The principle of conservation of mass and energy states that:

The total mass and energy in a system is always the same.

In other words, if some mass is lost, as in nuclear reactions, an equivalent amount of energy is created.

Check your understanding

1. What is the process by which energy is produced by the Sun?

2. Briefly explain what happens during the process described in question 1.

3. How does the process described in question 1 differ from burning a fuel like wood?

Fun fact

Every second on the Sun, around 4 200 000 000 kg of mass is converted into energy. This sounds like a lot, but compared with the total mass of the Sun, which is 2×10^{30} kg, it actually is not very much. ($2 \times 10^{30} = 2$ with 30 zeroes after it!) The Sun will continue to burn for billions of years to come.

Key terms

nuclear energy energy obtained when the nuclei of atoms undergo change

nuclear fusion the joining of two small nuclei to make one larger nucleus, with the loss of a small amount of mass

nuclear fission the division of one nucleus to form two smaller nuclei, with the loss of a small amount of mass

Energy transformations

We are learning how to:

- describe different non-renewable energy sources, including fossil fuels.

Non-renewable energy sources >>>

The sources of energy we use can be divided into two groups: renewable and non-renewable. If the energy source can be renewed by natural processes as fast as people use it, then it is renewable. If it cannot be renewed at this rate, then it is non-renewable.

Some sources of energy take many millions of years to form. People use the sources of energy up far more quickly than they can be replaced by nature. For this reason, these sources of energy are called non-renewable sources of energy.

Crude oil is not itself a useful source of energy but it is a raw material from which many fuels and other useful chemicals are made.

Natural gas is often found with crude oil. It is widely used for cooking and heating.

Coal is an important fuel in power stations for generating electricity. In Trinidad and Tobago, natural gas is used to generate electricity.

FIG 11.32 The oil refinery at Point a Pierre, Trinidad and Tobago, is one of the largest oil refineries in the Caribbean. It processes crude oil produced offshore to create many useful products such as gasoline and other chemicals

FIG 11.33 Natural gas is a fossil fuel that is widely used for cooking

FIG 11.34 Coal

Crude oil, natural gas and coal are sometimes described as fossil fuels. They formed deep in the ground from the decomposition of plant and animal remains. The rocks that contain crude oil, natural gas and coal often contain fossils of the organisms from which the fuels formed.

Fossil fuels are used to provide electricity. These types of power station produce large amounts of electricity but they have certain disadvantages.

FIG 11.35 An open-cast coal mine has a large impact on the environment

Some disadvantages of fossil fuels are:

- removing a fossil fuel from the ground may damage the environment

- fossil fuels produce atmospheric pollutants when the fuels are burned

- only limited amounts of fossil fuels remain in the ground.

Check your understanding

1. Table 11.3 gives a rough estimate of how many years reserves of each fossil fuel will last. The values were obtained by dividing the known reserves of each fuel by the amount currently extracted each year.

Fossil fuel	Number of years the fuel is expected to last
coal	113
crude oil	53
natural gas	56

TABLE 11.3

   a) Reserves of which fossil fuel:
   i) are likely to run out first?
   ii) are likely to last for the longest time?
   b) Suggest one reason why these estimates may not be accurate.

Fun fact

The fuel for nuclear power stations is uranium.

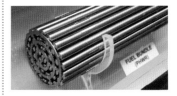

FIG 11.36 Uranium fuel is contained in metal fuel rods

Uranium is also a non-renewable source of energy, but reserves of nuclear fuels will last much longer than reserves of fossil fuels.

Renewable energy sources

We are learning how to:

- describe different renewable energy sources.

Renewable energy sources

Some sources of energy are continually replaced by natural processes at the same rate as they are used. These are called renewable sources of energy, and they will never run out.

Fresh water falls as rain and gathers in streams and rivers. Barriers called **dams** can be built across large rivers. The water is allowed to pass through tunnels in the dam wall, where it drives turbines to make electricity called **hydroelectricity**.

The Sun provides heat and light. **Solar panels** can turn solar energy into electricity.

In some parts of the world, **geothermal energy** is obtained from hot rocks near the surface. The energy converts water to steam, which can be used for heating and also to generate electricity.

On the coast, the water level rises and falls twice each day due to the movement of the tides. A tidal power station traps the water behind a barrier (a **tidal barrage**) at high tide and allows it to flow out at low tide. As the water flows out, electricity is generated from the **tidal energy**.

FIG 11.37 A dam holds back water

FIG 11.38 Solar panels gather energy from sunlight

FIG 11.39 Geothermal energy comes from the ground

FIG 11.40 A tidal barrage traps water at high tide

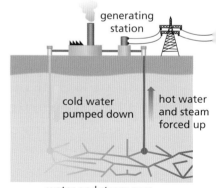

generating station

cold water pumped down

hot water and steam forced up

water and steam pass through cracks in the rocks

FIG 11.41 Geothermal energy – cold water is heated as it passes through the hot rock

Wind is the flow of air from one place to another. Wind has movement energy that can be used to do work. **Wind turbines** use energy from the wind to generate electricity.

FIG 11.42 Wind drives wind turbines, which generate electricity

Renewable sources of energy have both advantages and disadvantages.

Some advantages of renewable energy sources are:

- The energy is free.
- The energy will never run out.
- Making use of renewable energy causes relatively little environmental damage.
- Some devices are cheap to buy and install.
- Some devices are better suited than a power station to satisfying the needs of a small community.

Some disadvantages are:

- Some sources are not available all the time; for example, wind turbines only generate electricity when there is wind to drive them.
- Some sources provide relatively little energy; for example, it takes a large number of wind turbines to produce the same amount of electricity as a fossil-fuel-powered power station.
- Some sources are not suitable for all countries; for example, hydroelectricity is no use in a country where there are no fast-flowing rivers.

Check your understanding

1. From the examples of renewable energy sources given above, select the following, giving reasons for your choice:

    a) one source that would be suitable in Trinidad and Tobago
    b) one source that would not be suitable in Trinidad and Tobago.

Fun fact

Solar water heaters use heat from the Sun, which is a renewable source of energy.

FIG 11.43 Solar water heaters

Key terms

dam a wall built across a river to control the flow of water

hydroelectricity electricity that is generated using energy from moving water

solar panel a device that converts sunlight into electricity

geothermal energy heat energy that is obtained from the ground

tidal barrage a barrier across a tidal river to trap the water that flows in as the tide rises

tidal energy energy associated with the rise and fall of the sea level due to tides

wind turbine a device that converts kinetic energy from the wind into electricity

Biofuels

We are learning how to:

- describe different types of biofuel
- make a biogas generator.

Biofuels »»

Biofuels are the result of energy stored by photosynthesis – either directly, like **wood** obtained from trees, or indirectly, by animals eating plants and producing dung. They are an important source of energy in some countries.

In Africa, many people rely on wood and on **charcoal**, which is made from wood, as fuels to cook their food. Wood can be a renewable source of energy if new trees are planted to replace those that are used for fuel.

Biogas is an impure form of methane, made by fermenting animal dung. Biogas units can be small and serve one family, or they can be large and serve a small village. What remains of the dung after gas production can be used as a fertiliser in the soil to help crops grow and give better yields.

FIG 11.44 Wood is an important fuel in many parts of Africa

FIG 11.45 Biogas is a renewable source of energy

Activity 11.7

Making a biogas generator

Here is what you need:

- plastic drink bottles (2 litre or larger) × 2
- dung (goat or cow but not chicken)
- thick polythene bag (such as from a box of wine)
- stopper × 3 (two 2-hole stoppers and one 1-hole stopper to fit the bottles and bag)
- plastic tubing
- weak solution of sodium hydroxide
- small clamp like a sprung clothes peg.

Here is what you should do:

1. Arrange the bottles and bag as shown in Fig 11.46. You might need a stand and clamp to support the bag.

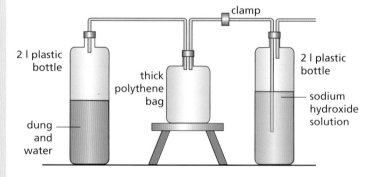

FIG 11.46

2. Half fill the left-hand bottle with a mixture of dung and water. Half fill the right-hand bottle with sodium hydroxide solution.

3. Place stoppers in the bottles and polythene bag, and connect them with rubber tubing.

4. Place a clamp on the tube leading from the polythene bag to the bottle containing sodium hydroxide solution.

5. Put the apparatus somewhere warm and leave it for several days.

6. When the bag starts to swell up, remove the clamp and push bubbles of biogas through the sodium hydroxide solution.

7. With the help of your teacher, try to light the gas.

Notice that the biogas generator initially produces carbon dioxide, which is not flammable. When the biogas is bubbled through sodium hydroxide, the carbon dioxide should be removed. The sodium hydroxide container also prevents any flashback once the gas is lit. If your gas does not light first time, let the gas build up for another day and then try again.

Ethanol is a biofuel made by fermenting sugar or other plant material.

In some countries, ethanol is mixed with gasoline or used as an alternative fuel to gasoline for road vehicles.

FIG 11.47 Ethanol can be used as an alternative to gasoline

Fun fact

Biodiesel is a renewable alternative to the diesel fuel obtained from crude oil. Biodiesel is made from vegetable and animal oils, and is therefore a biofuel.

FIG 11.48

Check your understanding

1. Charcoal is an important fuel in the Caribbean, where it is used to cook food.

   FIG 11.49 Charcoal

   a) Carry out some research to find out how charcoal is obtained.

   b) Explain why charcoal is a biofuel.

Key terms

biofuel a fuel obtained from living matter

wood a fuel obtained from trees

charcoal a fuel obtained by heating wood in the absence of air

biogas a fuel gas made by the fermentation of animal waste

ethanol a chemical made by the fermentation of sugar that can be used as a fuel

Transforming energy

We are learning how to:

- investigate the transformation of energy from one form to another.

Transforming energy from one form into others »

There are many examples in everyday life where one form of energy is changed into others. These changes are called **energy transformations** and they take place when work is done.

When fuels burn, the chemical potential energy they contain is converted into heat energy and light energy.

FIG 11.50 Energy transformations take place in our bodies

FIG 11.51 When fuels burn they produce heat and light energy

We can show this as a flow diagram:

chemical energy ⟶ heat energy + light energy

The food that we eat contains chemical potential energy. It is broken down to provide heat energy to maintain body temperature, and for other needs such as movement:

chemical energy ⟶ heat energy + kinetic energy

In an electric cell, chemicals produce electricity:

chemical energy ⟶ electrical energy

FIG 11.52 Electric cells

Many electrical appliances transform electrical energy into other forms of energy.

An electric iron transforms electrical energy into heat energy:

electrical energy ⟶ heat energy

FIG 11.53 An electric iron

Often, the transformation of electrical energy involves the production of more than one form of energy. For example, a television produces light and sound. It also produces a small amount of heat, which is lost to the surrounding air:

$$\text{electrical} \longrightarrow \text{light} + \text{sound} + \text{heat}$$
$$\text{energy} \quad\quad \text{energy} \quad \text{energy} \quad \text{energy}$$

FIG 11.54 A television set

Activity 11.8

Investigating energy transformations

Here is what you need:

- devices or pictures of devices to examine.

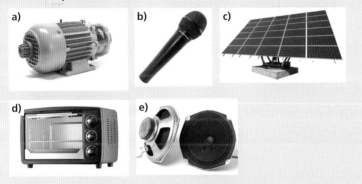

FIG 11.55

Here is what you should do:

1. For each device, decide how it changes energy.

2. Draw a flow diagram to show the energy transformation.

3. Make a classroom display to illustrate energy transformations.

Check your understanding

1. Draw a flow diagram to show the energy transformations that take place in each of the following:

    a) an electric kettle
    b) a bicycle bell
    c) a burning candle.

Key term

energy transformation a process in which one form of energy is changed into other forms of energy

Law of conservation of energy

We are learning how to:

- Measure the energy efficiency of different light bulbs.

Law of conservation of energy ➤➤➤

In the previous topic we learned how energy can be transformed from one form into others. It is often the case that an input of one form of energy can result in the output of two or more different forms of energy.

No matter what the nature of the energy transformations, the amounts of energy input and energy output are related by the **law of conservation of energy**:

> The law of conservation of energy states that energy can neither be created nor destroyed but only changed from one form to another.

In other words, whenever an energy transformation takes place the total energy output is always exactly equal to the total amount of energy input:

$$\text{energy input} = \text{energy output}$$

It might sometimes appear that a device does not follow the law of conservation of energy.

The purpose of a lamp is to provide light energy. However, for every 100 J of electrical energy a traditional incandescent lamp receives it only produces 10 J of light energy. Does this mean that 90 J of energy has been lost?

100 J electrical energy ⇒ 10 J light energy + 90 J heat energy

                    useful energy   wasted energy

  energy input   energy output

This energy has not been lost but has been transformed into another form of energy, heat, which we don't want. The terms '**useful energy**' and '**wasted energy**' are sometimes used to describe the forms of output energy. In the case of a traditional incandescent lamp, light energy is useful energy while heat energy is wasted energy.

Efficiency

The proportion of input energy that a device converts into useful output energy is called its **efficiency**.

The efficiency of the traditional incandescent lamp above is:

$$\frac{10\,\text{J}}{100\,\text{J}} = 0.1$$

FIG 11.56 A lamp provides light energy

Fun fact

The term 'lost energy' should never be used to describe unwanted forms of energy resulting from an energy transformation. Lost implies that the energy has been destroyed, which is not the case.

Notice that efficiency has no units since it is a ratio of two amounts of energy. Efficiency can also be expressed as a percentage simply by multiplying by 100, so 0.1 is equivalent to 10% efficient.

In theory, the highest efficiency a device can have is 1.0 or 100%, but in reality efficiency is always less than 1. All devices produce some wasted energy, often in the form of heat and/or sound energy.

Activity 11.9

Investigating the efficiency of different electric light sources

Work in groups of four.

Here is what you should do:

1. In your group, research into the efficiency and cost of different types of electric lights which are now available. You already know that a filament lamp is about 10% efficient. Find out about the other types of lamps shown in Fig 11.57.

FIG 11.57 Different types of electric lamps

2. More efficient electric lighting is often more expensive to buy but is cheaper to run and lasts longer before needing to be replaced. Use the information you gather to identify the cheapest way to light a home over a period of one year.

FIG 11.58 An electric drill produces kinetic energy, heat energy and sound energy

Check your understanding

1. For every 100 J of electrical energy a drill receives it produces 62 J of kinetic energy, 27 J of heat energy and x J of sound energy.

   a) Calculate the value of x.

   b) Draw a flow diagram for the energy transformations that take place in the drill.

   c) How much of the 100 J of electrical energy is transformed into:

      i) useful energy?   ii) wasted energy?

   d) What is the percentage efficiency of the drill?

Key terms

law of conservation of energy during an energy transformation energy is neither created nor destroyed

useful energy output energy in a form that is useful for the desired purpose

wasted energy output energy that is not useful for the desired purpose

efficiency proportion of input energy that a device converts into useful output energy

Sankey diagrams

We are learning how to:

- use Sankey diagrams to describe energy transformations.

Sankey diagrams 〉〉

A Sankey diagram is a way of showing the proportions of different forms of **energy** produced during an **energy transformation**. The proportion can be shown as an actual number of joules (J) or simply as a percentage of the starting energy.

Remember that energy can neither be created nor destroyed. When drawing a diagram to show an energy transformation, the amount of energy input will be exactly the same as the sum of the forms of energy output.

For example, in a filament light bulb, 90% of the electrical energy is transformed into heat energy and 10% is transformed into light energy. Filament bulbs are not very efficient at producing light. Most of the electrical energy is transformed into heat, which is why light bulbs get hot.

Fig 11.59 shows how the energy transformations in a filament light bulb are represented in a **Sankey diagram**. The width of the arrows is in proportion to the heat energy and light energy produced.

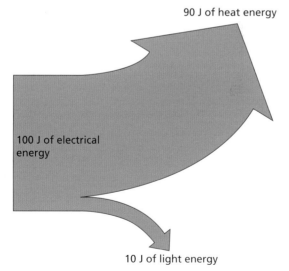

90 J of heat energy

100 J of electrical energy

10 J of light energy

FIG 11.59 A Sankey diagram for the energy transformations in a filament light bulb

Drawing a Sankey diagram

Here is what you need:

- squared paper
- ruler.

Here is what you should do:

1. Read the following information about a hairdryer:

   When a hairdryer is operated, 10% of the electrical energy is transformed to kinetic energy to drive the fan, 40% is converted into sound and 50% into heat.

2. Start with a line on the left that is 10 squares high to represent 100% of the energy.

3. Draw a Sankey diagram to represent the information about the hairdryer.

We can also draw Sankey diagrams for energy transformations that produce more than two forms of energy.

Fig 11.60 shows how the energy obtained by burning a fuel in a power station is transformed into other forms of energy. From this diagram we can see that less than half the energy in the fuel is transformed into electricity.

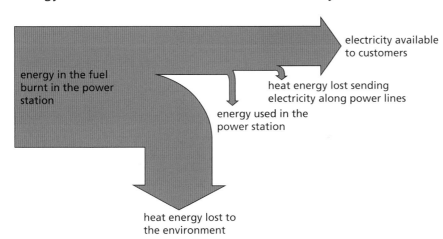

FIG 11.60 A Sankey diagram for the energy transformations in a fossil fuel power station

Fun fact

Sankey diagrams are named after Henry Sankey. He first used this kind of diagram in 1898 to show the energy transformations in a steam engine.

Key terms

energy the ability to do work

energy transformation a process in which one form of energy is changed into other forms of energy

Sankey diagram a diagram used to show energy transformations

Check your understanding

1. Use the Sankey diagram in Fig 11.60 to estimate what percentage of the energy contained in the fuel burnt in the power station is transformed in the different ways shown.

Conservation of energy (1)

We are learning how to:

- describe how the Government is planning to make use of more renewable sources of energy.

Conservation of energy – the Government

The population of the world is growing every day, and people are continually looking for ways to raise their standard of living. This creates an ever-increasing demand for **energy**.

FIG 11.61 World demand for energy increases every year

Energy conservation may be considered at the level of countries and also at the level of individuals. In considering energy conservation, we are really looking at ways of making more use of renewable energy sources in order to conserve those energy sources that are not renewable.

Trinidad and Tobago is the largest producer of oil and natural gas in the Caribbean, and the world's sixth largest exporter of liquid natural gas (LNG). Both crude oil and natural gas are non-renewable sources of energy; reserves of these resources will eventually run out.

An economy based on non-renewable energy sources will not be **sustainable** in the years to come. Trinidad and Tobago is therefore committed to moving towards obtaining more energy from renewable sources.

One likely source of renewable energy in Trinidad and Tobago is wind power. In 2013, the Government set up the Wind Resource Assessment Programme (WRAP).

WRAP aims to identify five locations on the east coast of the country that are best suited to the construction of **wind farms**. The east coast is preferred to the west coast because it receives strong winds from the Atlantic Ocean.

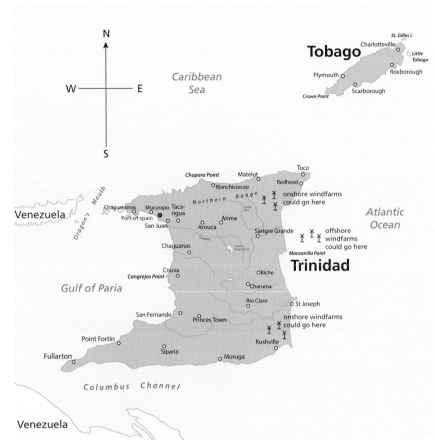

FIG 11.62 Map of Trinidad and Tobago

FIG 11.63 A wind farm

> ### Fun fact
>
> Not everybody agrees that wind farms are a good thing. Wind farms harness a renewable source of energy and do not pollute the atmosphere, but some people think they are eyesores that ruin the natural beauty of the landscape.

A wind farm is a collection of **wind turbines**. Each wind turbine uses kinetic energy from the wind to generate electricity:

kinetic energy ⟶ electrical energy

Check your understanding

1. Why is the wind a renewable energy source?

2. What energy transformation takes place in a wind turbine?

3. What is the collective name for a number of wind turbines?

4. Why is the development of wind power in Trinidad and Tobago focused on the east coast?

5. Give one advantage and one disadvantage of a wind turbine.

Key terms

energy the ability to do work

sustainable describes a process that can be kept at a certain level or rate for as long as we want it

wind farm a collection of two or more wind turbines

wind turbine a device that converts kinetic energy from the wind into electricity

Conservation of energy (2)

We are learning how to:

- conserve energy ourselves by making better choices.

Conservation of energy – the individual ⟫⟫

Governments decide a country's energy policy, but this does not mean that the individual does not have a role to play in conserving energy.

Petrol and diesel are obtained from crude oil, which is a non-renewable source of energy. Every time we drive somewhere we use more of that energy source and also add to atmospheric pollution. There are times when people need to use cars and lorries, but there are also times when people can save energy by walking or cycling.

FIG 11.64 Cycling conserves energy and does not pollute the environment

Traditional light bulbs contain a metal filament that glows white hot to produce light. Light bulbs are very inefficient. Around 90% of the electricity they consume is wasted as heat energy.

Modern energy-saving bulbs work in a different way. Energy-saving light bulbs are often more expensive than traditional light bulbs, but they are still better value. They last longer and give out the same amount of light, but use less electricity.

Energy can be conserved by changing to energy-saving bulbs and also by remembering to switch lights off when you leave a room.

FIG 11.65 Modern bulbs use less electrical energy than filament lamps

Activity 11.11

How can I conserve energy?

Work in groups of four.

Here is what you should do:

1. In your group, discuss how you might be able to conserve energy. Make a list of your ideas.

2. Nominate one person in the group to be the spokesperson and share your group's ideas with the rest of the class.

Much of the energy that countries consume is used when manufacturing materials. If people used less materials, there would be a significant saving in energy. Here are three things you can do – the 'three Rs':

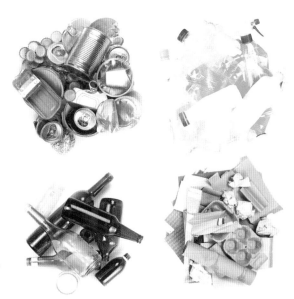

- **Reduce** the quantity of manufactured goods you use. For example, do you really need a bag every time you buy something at the store?

- **Reuse** some items instead of buying new ones. For example, if you need a bag to carry things home from the shop, take the bag you were given last week. You do not need a new one every time.

FIG 11.66 Examples of materials that can be recycled

- **Recycle** materials so they can be made into new objects. If you have empty glass or plastic containers, or metal cans, those materials can be reused. Do not just throw them away.

Check your understanding

1. Table 11.4 gives some information about an old type of electric light bulb and a modern energy-saving bulb.

Type of bulb	Cost to buy	Cost to light the bulb for 10 hours each day	Number of days before needs to be replaced
old	$3	$1	100 days
modern energy-saving	$15	$0.40	300 days

TABLE 11.4

a) How much more expensive is it to buy a modern bulb than an old-style bulb?

b) For how many days would a person have to use a modern bulb in order to save the difference in the cost between an old bulb and a modern bulb?

c) How much would a person save lighting a room for 300 days using modern bulbs rather than old bulbs?

Fun fact

In some countries, people place different kinds of waste material in different bins so they can easily be recycled.

FIG 11.67

Key terms

conserve to make something last longer by using less of it

reduce to make smaller

reuse to use an object again

recycle to use the material from an object to make a new object

Review of Forces and energy

Forces

- Forces can:
  - change the motion of an object
  - change the direction of a moving object
  - change the shape of an object.

- Forces can be of two types:
  - contact forces
  - non-contact forces.

- Examples of contact forces include friction and buoyancy.

- Examples of non-contact forces include gravity, electrostatic forces and magnetism.

- Friction is a force on surfaces when they move over each other.

- Friction when an object moves in water or in air is called water resistance and air resistance, respectively.

- Streamlining involves shaping objects so that they have as little resistance as possible.

- The unit of force is the newton, which has the symbol N.

- Forces have both magnitude (size) and direction.

- A force can be represented in a diagram by an arrow in which:
  - the magnitude of the force is indicated by the length of the arrow
  - the direction of the force is given by the direction of the arrow.

- A resultant force is the single force obtained by adding two or more forces.

- Weight is the force acting on an object towards the ground due to the pull of gravity. The weight of an object can be calculated using the equation:

$$\text{weight} = \text{mass} \times \text{acceleration due to gravity}$$

- The acceleration due to gravity, g, has the value 9.81 m/s^2 on Earth. The value is sometimes taken as 10 m/s^2 in order to simplify calculations.

- The mass of an object will be the same anywhere in the universe, but the weight of an object will vary from planet to planet, according to the different gravitational forces.

- Pressure is the ratio of a force to the area over which it is applied. The equation is:

$$\text{pressure} = \text{force/area}$$

- The unit of pressure is the pascal, which has the symbol Pa.

- A pressure of 1 pascal is equivalent to a force of 1 newton acting over an area of 1 square metre.

- Everyday examples of the application of pressure include: fizzy drinks, inflating bicycle tyres, spraying with hosepipes, blood pressure, thumb tacks and water birds.

Energy

- Energy is the ability to do work.

- Energy in different contexts is described as different forms of energy.

- Forms of energy include: heat, light, sound, electrical energy, chemical energy, nuclear energy, potential energy and kinetic energy.

- Potential energy is energy that is stored in some way and includes: gravitational potential energy, chemical potential energy and elastic potential energy.

- Kinetic energy is the energy that objects have when they move.

- In a swinging pendulum, energy is converted between gravitational potential energy and kinetic energy.

- Nuclear energy is the result of changes to the structure of atoms. It is the source of energy in the Sun and in nuclear power stations.

- Non-renewable energy sources are those that are not replaced by nature at the same rate as they are used up. They include coal, crude oil and natural gas.

- Renewable energy sources are those that are replaced by nature at the same rate as they are used up. They include hydroelectric energy (flowing water), solar energy, geothermal energy, tidal energy and wind energy.

- Biofuels are the result of energy stored by photosynthesis either directly, for example in wood obtained from trees, or indirectly, for example by animals eating plants and producing dung. Biofuels include biogas, wood, charcoal and ethanol.

- Energy can be transformed from one form into others. When this happens, work is done.

- The law of conservation of energy states that energy can neither be created nor destroyed but only changed from one form to another.

- The efficiency of a device is the proportion of input energy that is converted into useful output energy.

- Energy transformations can be shown as Sankey diagrams.

- The world is moving towards a greater use of renewable sources of energy as reserves of non-renewable energy sources are used up.

- Trinidad and Tobago is currently investigating the possibility of building wind farms at some locations on the east coast of the country.

- Individual people can make a significant contribution to reducing a the country's demand for energy.

Review questions on Forces and energy

1. Fig 11.68 shows the directions of three forces acting on a racing car.

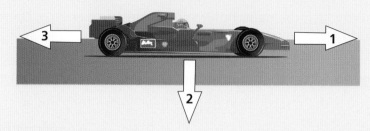

FIG 11.68

   a) In which direction would an applied force:
      i) slow the car down?
      ii) hold the car on the road?
      iii) speed the car up?
   b) Say whether each force is a push or a pull.

2. Fig 11.69 shows a book with two forces acting on it.

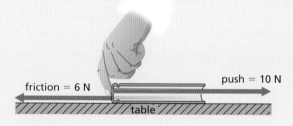

friction = 6 N   push = 10 N

table

FIG 11.69

   a) What unit does 'N' represent?
   b) What is the significance of the arrow that represents a force?
   c) What is the resultant force on the book?
   d) Are these examples of contact forces or non-contact forces?

3. The mass of a beaker containing some powder is measured on an electronic balance (Fig 11.70).

   a) What is the reading on the balance?
   b) After removing the powder, the mass of the empty beaker is 119.87 g. What is the mass of the powder?
   c) What is the mass of the powder expressed in milligrams?

1 2 7 · 5 3 g

FIG 11.70

4. **a)** What is the pressure exerted when a force of 400 N acts on an area of 20 cm²?

 b) Over what area must a force of 500 N act in order to exert a pressure of 10 cm²?

 c) A cube of sides 5 cm exerts a pressure of 0.5 N/cm² when placed on a table. What is the weight of the cube?

5. Marie is a downhill skier.

 a) Why does Marie not sink into the snow when she is wearing skis, but she does sink when she is wearing her ordinary shoes?

 b) Why does Marie rub wax on the underneath of her skis?

 c) Why does Marie crouch down when she is skiing?

FIG 11.71

6. Table 11.5 shows some of the world's energy sources. They are arranged in order of the total amount of energy they provide.

Energy source	Relative amount of energy provided
oil	most energy supplied
natural gas	
coal	↓
nuclear	
hydroelectric	
wind farms	least energy supplied

TABLE 11.5

 a) From this table give:

  i) a non-renewable source of energy

  ii) a renewable source of energy.

 b) What is meant by a 'non-renewable energy source'?

 c) Name one other large-scale source of energy not given in the table.

 d) If a similar table was drawn up in 100 years from now, suggest one way in which it would be different.

7. The following pie chart shows the proportions of energy a country gets from different sources.

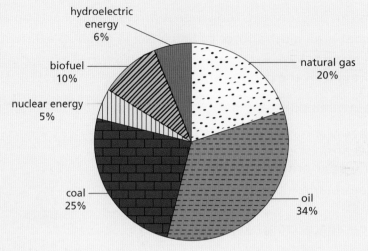

FIG 11.72

a) Which source provides:

i) the most energy?

ii) the least energy?

b) Explain why hydroelectric energy can be described as a renewable source of energy.

c) Explain how the energy in biofuels originally came from the Sun.

8. The following energy transformations take place in different devices. For each transformation, name one example of a suitable device.

a) electrical energy ⟶ heat energy

b) chemical energy ⟶ heat energy

c) electrical energy ⟶ kinetic energy

d) kinetic energy ⟶ electrical energy

e) electrical energy ⟶ light energy

f) electrical energy ⟶ sound energy

9. A dairy farmer has decided to conserve energy by using a renewable energy source. He has three options:

a) biogas – he has cattle dung from his dairy cows

b) hydroelectricity – a small river flows through his land

c) wind turbine – there is a hill on his land where a wind turbine could be built.

Briefly explain how each of these could provide energy. Give one disadvantage of each, apart from the cost of starting up.

10. A wind turbine is to be built at Windy Cove. The following graphs show details about the conditions and the electricity that would be generated.

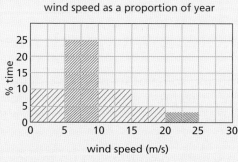

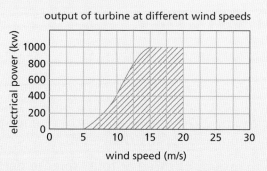

FIG 11.73

a) What is the maximum number of kilowatts of electricity the wind turbine will be able to generate?

b) Suggest a reason why:

   i) no electricity would be generated when the wind speed falls below 5 metres per second (m/s)

   ii) the wind turbine would be prevented from rotating when the wind speed rises above 20 m/s.

c) Predict for how many days the wind turbine would generate electricity.

Providing your school with energy

1. The Head Teacher wants your school to start producing some of its own electricity from suitable renewable energy sources. The target is to produce 30% of the school's electricity by 2020. The Head Teacher needs technical advice on the type of device the school should adopt to achieve this.

   Work in groups of three or four. You are part of a school committee set up to look into this issue and make recommendations. The tasks are:

   - write a PowerPoint presentation in which you recommend which device the school should adopt, and explain the reasons for your choice
   - build a prototype of the device, which can be located at the designated location at the school and used to test the viability of your recommendation.

2. When carrying out your research and making your recommendations you need to be mindful of the constraints and limitations associated with each type of device. The device that produces the most electricity might not be the one that is most suitable for the school to use. What factors should you consider in your research and recommendations? Discuss in your group and make a list.

3. Research renewable sources of energy that can be used to produce electricity. Use the information in Topic 11.9 to guide you. You might also find useful information by looking up other phrases like 'solar furnace' and 'wave energy' on the internet. What renewable sources of energy are being used or will soon be used in schools and colleges in different parts of Trinidad and Tobago?

FIG 11.74 Solar furnace at Odeillo, France

FIG 11.75 Wave energy transformer floats

4. Consider the suitability of the different devices available for use within your school. Be mindful of the constraints and limitations associated with each type of device. Consider issues such as:

   - How much electricity is the school hoping to produce from renewable energy sources? i.e. How much electricity does the school use each year and what is 30% of this amount?

- Which devices will be able to supply this amount of electricity?
- Is the location and the fabric of the school appropriate for a particular device? For example, is the school in a sheltered spot that receives little wind? Do the school buildings have roofs where solar panels could be positioned?
- Which devices are practical options in terms of the cost of buying them and maintaining them?

Decide which renewable energy source you are going to recommend. Prepare reasons for your choice.

5. Build a model of a device that uses the renewable source of energy you have chosen. For example, you might build:

   - A solar panel that is connected in a circuit with a light-emitting diode (LED) which lights up when the sun shines on the solar panel.
   - An electric motor with a propeller attached to the spindle. When the propeller is driven around by the wind the motor becomes a generator and produces an electric current that can be detected using an ammeter.

FIG 11.76 A wind turbine

Since wind and sunlight are not available every hour of the day, you should think about how electricity can be stored by a capacitor on your prototype, and by a battery on the actual device.

6. Test your model to determine if it can carry out its designed function.

   - Place your device in the location you have decided is suitable for it and monitor the amount of electricity being produced over a week.
   - Compare this with the amount of electricity the school hopes to produce and decide how your prototype might be scaled up to meet this amount.

FIG 11.77 Solar panel at Parvati Girl's High School

   - Consider ways in which you might improve the efficiency of your prototype.

7. Give a PowerPoint presentation to the class on what you have found and what you will recommend. You should be prepared to explain why you are recommending this particular renewable energy source.

   Discuss possible improvements with the class, and refine your recommendation and the design of your prototype as necessary.

Index

Acknowledgements

pp6–7: NASA, pp6: Science Photo Library/Getty Images, pp7: Glow Wellness/Getty Images, pp7 (BL): LOUISE BARKER/AMERICAN INSTITUTE OF PHYSICS/SCIENCE PHOTO LIBRARY, pp7 (BR): The Print Collector/Alamy, pp9: ZUMA Press/Alamy, pp10: Volt Collection/Shutterstock, pp12: wavebreakmedia/Shutterstock, pp13: Don Mason/Getty Images, pp14: IgorGolovniov/Shutterstock, pp18: Horiyan/Shutterstock, pp18: Tim Masters/Shutterstock, pp18: Datacraft Co Ltd/Getty Images, pp18: Blinka/Shutterstock, pp18: SCIENCE PHOTO LIBRARY, pp18: Matthew Cole/Shutterstock, pp18: Gavs_ira/Fotolia, pp18: Yurko Gud/Shutterstock, pp18: 33333/Shutterstock, pp18: Matthew Cole/Shutterstock, pp18: litchima/Shutterstock, pp18: Jim Hughes/Shutterstock, pp18: Photo Melon/Shutterstock, pp19: sciencephotos/Alamy, pp19: sciencephotos/Alamy, pp21: Voisin/Phanie/REX, pp26–27: Martin Shields / Alamy, pp26: Suppakij1017/Shutterstock, pp28: revers/Shutterstock, pp30: icefront/istockphoto, pp32: PRILL/Shutterstock, pp37: icefront/istockphoto, pp38: Andrey_Popov/Shutterstock, pp39: Sciencephotos/Alamy, pp39: Yulia-Bogdanova/Shutterstock, pp39 : Matthew Mawson/Alamy, pp40: Sergey Melnikov/Shutterstock, pp40: Mega Pixel/Shutterstock, pp40: Andrey Burmakin/Shutterstock, pp40: Vilax/Shutterstock, pp40: JOE KLAMAR/AFP/Getty Images, pp42: Busypix/iStockphoto, pp43: AlexKol Photography/Shutterstock, pp43: IS_ImageSource/iStockphoto, pp43: Anzhely.K/Shutterstock, pp43: HamsterMan/Shutterstock, pp46–47: Pakhnyushchy/Shutterstock, pp46: Sam Edwards/Getty Images, pp46: Stillfx/Shutterstock, pp47: Gerd Guenther/Science Photo Library, pp47: Pakhnyushchy/Shutterstock, pp47: JPL-Caltech/NASA, pp48: Sahani Photography/Shutterstock, pp48: Tim Laman/Getty Images, pp50: De Agostini Picture Library/Getty Images, pp51: hadkhanong/Shutterstock, pp51: Image Source/Getty Images, pp52: WildPictures/Alamy, pp53: Cathlyn Melloan/Getty Images, pp53: Cordelia Molloy/Science Photo Library, pp53: Joe Petersburger/National Geographic Creative/Getty Images, pp54: Morales/Getty Images, pp54: M. Krofel Wildlife/Alamy, pp54: Matt Jeppson/Shutterstock, pp54: The Washington Post/Getty Images, pp55: Robert Harding Picture Library Ltd/Alamy, pp55: Musat/iStockphoto, pp56: Elenamiv/Shutterstock, pp56: Platteboone/iStockphoto, pp56: Polarpx/Shutterstock, pp57: Tom Uhlman/Alamy, pp57: Dreamstime, pp57: FLPA/Alamy, pp57: Bob Gibbons /Alamy, pp58: Visuals Unlimited/Encyclopedia/Corbis, pp59: Zhukov/Shutterstock, pp59: Tim Laman/Getty Images, pp61: Fir Mamat/Alamy, pp61: Arco Images GmbH/Alamy, pp60: AlexGreenArt/Shutterstock, pp60: Johann Schumacher/Getty Images, pp61: Andrew McRobb/Getty Images, pp60: COLIN VARNDELL/SCIENCE PHOTO LIBRARY, pp62-63: DR GOPAL MURTI/SCIENCE PHOTO LIBRARY, pp62: Glowimages/Getty Images, pp62: DR GOPAL MURTI/SCIENCE PHOTO LIBRARY, pp62: Biophoto Associates/SCIENCE PHOTO LIBRARY, pp62: Dennis Kunkel Microscopy/Visuals Unlimited/Corbis, pp63: KEVIN & BETTY COLLINS, VISUALS UNLIMITED /SCIENCE PHOTO LIBRARY, pp63: OHN DURHAM/SCIENCE PHOTO LIBRARY, pp63: Trinochka/Shutterstock, pp76: BIOPHOTO ASSOCIATES/Photo Researchers RM/Getty Images, pp63: Waj/Shutterstock, pp63: SINCLAIR STAMMERS/SCIENCE PHOTO LIBRARY, pp65: GEORGE MUSIL, VISUALS UNLIMITED/SCIENCE PHOTO LIBRARY, pp66: Biophoto Associates/Getty Images, pp66: Ed Reschke/Getty Images, pp66: INNERSPACE IMAGING/SCIENCE PHOTO LIBRARY, pp66: Dr. Gladden Willis/Visuals Unlimited/Corbis, pp67: Ed Reschke/Getty Images, pp67: Heiti Paves/Shutterstock, pp67: UCSF/Getty Images, pp68: BIOPHOTO ASSOCIATES/SCIENCE PHOTO LIBRARY, pp70: DEA/P. CASTANO/Getty Images, pp70: Glow Cuisine/Getty Images, pp71: blickwinkel/Alamy, pp72: Visuals Unlimited/Corbis, pp73: FRANK FOX/SCIENCE PHOTO LIBRARY, pp74–75: DAVID MCCARTHY/Getty Images, pp76: Lebendkulturen.de/Shutterstock, pp76: Lebendkulturen.de/Shutterstock, pp77: Carolina Biological/Visuals Unlimited/Corbis, pp81: Amawasri Pakdara/Shutterstock, pp81: David R. Frazier Photolibrary/Alamy, pp87: momopixs/Shutterstock, pp90: POWER AND SYRED/SCIENCE PHOTO LIBRARY, pp90: Dr. Gladden Willis/Visuals Unlimited/Corbis, pp93: Dave and Sigrun Tollerton/Alamy, pp94: Ed Reschke/Getty Images, pp96–97: bluehand/Shutterstock, pp96: Joshua Resnick/Shutterstock, pp100: LaChouettePhoto/iStockphoto, pp104: Anthony Mercieca/Getty Images, pp105: BIOPHOTO ASSOCIATES/SCIENCE PHOTO LIBRARY, pp108: Elena Schweitzer/Shutterstock, pp109: Tiger Images/Shutterstock, pp110–112: steve estvanik/Shutterstock, pp110: Westend61/Getty Images, pp110: cowardlion/Shutterstock, pp110: Phanom Nuangchomphoo/Shutterstock, pp110: Wittybear/Shutterstock, pp110: a-plus image bank / Alamy, pp111: XXLPhoto/Shutterstock, pp111: CC STUDIO/SCIENCE PHOTO LIBRARY, pp111: Africa Studio/Shutterstock, pp111: Phillip Evans/Visuals Unlimited/Corbis, pp111: androver/Shutterstock, pp111: Henrik Sorensen/Getty Images, pp114: Alexander Mazurkevich/Shutterstock, pp114: prill/iStockphoto, pp114: Peter Zijlstra/Shutterstock, pp114: RIA NOVOSTI/Getty Images, pp114: bogdan ionescu/Shutterstock, pp115: Peter Burnett/iStockphoto, pp115: macrowildlife/Shutterstock, pp115: Kerstin Waurick/Getty Images, pp115: ANDREW LAMBERT PHOTOGRAPHY/SCIENCE PHOTO LIBRARY, pp118: bunhill/iStockphoto, pp118: Peter Gardner/Getty Images, pp118: klikk/iStockphoto, pp118: t3000/iStockphoto, pp118: Laborant/Shutterstock, pp118: VIPDesignUSA/iStockphoto, pp118: GVictoria/Shutterstock, pp120: Pixmann/Alamy, pp121: Joey Photo/Shutterstock, pp121: Cclickclick/Getty Images, pp121: Zkruger/Shutterstock, pp122: Bill Boch/Getty Images, pp126: Anthony Hall/Shutterstock, pp128: Claude Nuridsany/Marie Perennou/Science Photo Library, pp128: Charles D. Winter/Science Photo Library, pp129: Jeff J Daly/Alamy, pp129: Voisin/Phanie/REX, pp129: Andy Paradise/REX, pp130: Denis Tabler/Shutterstock, pp131: ABB Photo/Shutterstock, pp132–133: Andrey Burmakin/Shutterstock, pp132: 9comeback/Shutterstock, pp132: Fablok/Shutterstock, pp132: Bulent camci/Shutterstock, pp132: By Ian Miles-Flashpoint Pictures / Alamy, pp132: Ventin/Shutterstock, pp132: baitong333/Shutterstock, pp134: nevodka/Shutterstock, pp136: Print Collector/Getty Images, pp137: Alexander Dashewsky/Shutterstock, pp141: Science Photo Library, pp141: Science Photo Library, pp141: Science Photo Library, pp141: Science Photo Library, pp141: Science Photo Library, pp144–145: Magcom/Shutterstock, pp144: Martyn F. Chillmaid/Science Photo Library, pp145: ANDREW LAMBERT PHOTOGRAPHY/SCIENCE PHOTO LIBRARY, pp146: sciencephotos/Alamy, pp149: Lopatin Anton/Shutterstock, pp149: ANDREW MCCLENAGHAN/SCIENCE PHOTO LIBRARY, pp149: everything possible/Shutterstock, pp149: CHARLES D. WINTERS/SCIENCE PHOTO LIBRARY, pp156–157: Patryk Kosmider/Shutterstock, pp156: Dmitry Guzhanin/Shutterstock, pp156: Buzz Pictures/Alamy, pp157: wavebreakmedia/Shutterstock, pp157: Marvin del Cid/Getty Images, pp158: Michael Dwyer/Alamy, pp158: slovegrove/iStockphoto, pp158: Dmitry Kalinovsky/Shutterstock, pp159: Bob Weymouth/Alamy, pp160: Germanskydiver/Shutterstock, pp160: ID1974/Shutterstock, pp160: GAILLARDIN/LOOK AT SCIENCES/SCIENCE PHOTO LIBRARY, pp164: Maximilian Weinzierl/Alamy, pp164: Zorandim/Shutterstock, pp164: Gallo Images/Getty Images, pp165: Reuters, pp165: FPG/Getty Images, pp165: SuperStock/Getty Images, pp165: Stuart Hickling/Alamy, pp170: Taina Sohlman/Alamy, pp170: MARTYN F. CHILLMAID/SCIENCE PHOTO LIBRARY, pp170: CHARLES D. WINTERS/SCIENCE PHOTO LIBRARY, pp170: Andy Crawford/Getty Images, pp171: NASA, pp172: NASA, pp174: NASA, pp174: Johns Hopkins University Applied Physics Laboratory/Carnegie Institution of Washington/NASA, pp175: NASA, pp175: Alain Riazuelo/NASA, pp176: Image Source/Getty Images, pp176: penguenstok/Getty Images, pp177: marilyn barbone/Shutterstock, pp180: Naypong/Shutterstock, pp180: Cebas/Shutterstock, pp180: Julija Sapic/Shutterstock, pp180: LeventeGyori/Shutterstock, pp181: john shepherd/iStockphoto, pp181: Ivan Kuzmin/Alamy, pp181: Fotokostic/Shutterstock, pp181: Federico Scoppa/Corbis, pp182–183: SCIENCE PHOTO LIBRARY/SOHO/ESA/NASA, pp182: Pakhnyushchy/Shutterstock, pp183: Jorge Silva/REUTERS, pp183: Pindyurin Vasily/Shutterstock, pp183: Joe Raedle/Getty Images, pp183: Erdosain/istockphoto, pp183: AdamEdwards/Shutterstock, pp183: jokerpro/Shutterstock, pp182: NASA, pp184: William Berry/Shutterstock, pp184: Elena Pominova/Shutterstock, pp185: Jeff Foott/Getty Images, pp186: Premaphotos/Alamy, pp186: Peter de Clercq/Alamy, pp188: Greg Balfour Evans/Alamy, pp188: Berislav Kovacevic/Shutterstock, pp188: Yegor Korzh/Shutterstock, pp189: Stefano Tinti/Shuttestock, pp190: Adams Picture Library t/a apl/Alamy, pp190: NASA, pp192: Mike P Shepherd/Alamy, pp192: Art Directors & TRIP/Alamy, pp193: Alex Potemkin/Getty images, pp194: rangizzz/Shutterstock, pp194: MichaelUtech/iStockphoto, pp196: Shirley Bahadur, File/Ap Photo, pp196: Oleksiy Mark/Shutterstock, pp196: Joop Zandbergen/Shutterstock, pp197: Monty Rakusen/Getty images, pp197: MARK WILLIAMSON/SCIENCE PHOTO LIBRARY, pp198: avleMarjanovic/Shutterstock, pp198: wang song/Shutterstock, pp198: Laurence Gough/Shutterstock, pp198: DeAgostini/Getty Images, pp199: pedrosala/Shutterstock, pp199: Chukcha/Shutterstock, pp200: Horizons WWP/Alamy, pp200: Universal Images Group/Getty images, pp201: Jason Lindsey / Alamy, pp201: yingphoto/Shutterstock, pp202: Dutourdumonde Photography/Shutterstock, pp202: Ian Walton/Getty images, pp202: Konjushenko Vladimir/Shutterstock, pp202: Kattiya L /Shutterstock, pp203: Andrey Popov/Shutterstock, pp203: Theerawut_SS/Shutterstock, pp203: Ensuper/Shutterstock, pp203: Natalia Macheda/Shutterstock, pp203: CollinsChin/iStockphoto/, pp203: sciencephotos/Alamy, pp204: Sarunyu/Shutterstock, pp205: Chones/Shutterstock, pp205: Goodluz/Shutterstock, pp208: Neil Mitchell/Shutterstock, pp210: Images of Africa Photobank/Alamy, pp210: Hurst Photo/Shutterstock, pp211: Atelier_A/Shutterstock, pp211: Tomasz Makowski/Shutterstock, pp218: Arterra/UIG/Getty Images, pp218: Getty Images, pp218: Colin Underhill / Alamy Stock Photo, pp218: Per-Anders Pettersson/Getty Images.